Corporate Acquisitions and Mergers in Kazakhstan and Uzbekistan

Corporate Acquisitions and Mergers in Kazakhstan and Uzbekistan

Second Edition

Adlet Yerkinbayev
Joel Benjamin
Muborak Kambarova

Kinstellar

This book was originally published as a chapter in Corporate
Acquisitions and Mergers.

General Editor: Peter Begg

 Wolters Kluwer

Published by:
Kluwer Law International B.V.
PO Box 316
2400 AH Alphen aan den Rijn
The Netherlands
E-mail: lrs-sales@wolterskluwer.com
Website: www.wolterskluwer.com/en/solutions/kluwerlawinternational

Sold and distributed by:
Wolters Kluwer Legal & Regulatory U.S.
7201 McKinney Circle
Frederick, MD 21704
United States of America
E-mail: customer.service@wolterskluwer.com

DISCLAIMER: The material in this volume is in the nature of general comment only. It is not offered as advice on any particular matter and should not be taken as such. The editor and the contributing authors expressly disclaim all liability to any person with regard to anything done or omitted to be done, and with respect to the consequences of anything done or omitted to be done wholly or partly in reliance upon the whole or any part of the contents of this volume. No reader should act or refrain from acting on the basis of any matter contained in this volume without first obtaining professional advice regarding the particular facts and circumstances at issue. Any and all opinions expressed herein are those of the particular author and are not necessarily those of the editor or publisher of this volume.

Printed on acid-free paper

ISBN 978-94-035-4990-3

e-Book: ISBN 978-94-035-4331-4
web-PDF: ISBN 978-94-035-4341-3

Printed and bound by CPI Group (UK) Ltd, Croydon, CR0 4YY

Contents

Kinstellar

Kinstellar acts as a trusted legal counsel to leading investors across Emerging Europe and Central Asia. Its reputation for quality, excellence and integrity speaks for itself.

With offices in eleven jurisdictions and over 300 local and international lawyers, Kinstellar delivers consistent, joined-up legal advice and assistance across diverse regional markets – together with the know-how and experience to champion the client's interests while minimizing exposure to risk.

In Kazakhstan, Kinstellar has offices in Almaty and Nur-Sultan, which were launched in 2013 and 2018, respectively. Our Nur-Sultan office operates through Kinstellar Astana, an AIFC Participant which is a recognized company holding a licence for providing legal services on the territory of the Astana International Financial Centre.

Kinstellar's clients include leading international and regional corporations, banks and other financial institutions, state bodies, multilateral institutions, and international law firms with clients that require top-quality legal counsel in our jurisdictions. Kinstellar handles the most important and complex assignments for clients across diverse industries and business sectors.

The Kinstellar's lawyers are regularly ranked for their knowledge and quality of their client service by the reputed international legal directories, such as *Chambers and Partners*, *Legal 500*, and *IFLR 1000*.

Authors

Adlet Yerkinbayev is a partner and Joel Benjamin is the managing partner at Kinstellar in Kazakhstan. Both Adlet and Joel have been involved in a large number of high-profile M&A transactions. Adlet's practice focuses on M&A, capital markets and banking and finance. Over the years, Adlet has been involved in a large number of such transactions, in particular in the banking and telecommunications sectors in Kazakhstan. Joel Benjamin has been working in Kazakhstan since 1993. He has played a leading role in numerous transactions including bilateral and syndicated loans, trade finance, project finance, equity and debt capital market and M&A transactions.

Disclaimer

This document does not purport to contain a comprehensive summary of all the legal risks and issues in the legal areas it covers. It is to be used for general information only and cannot be relied upon as legal advice. No legal or business decision should be based solely on this document.

1 LOCAL ECONOMIC, POLITICAL AND CULTURAL ASPECTS

1.1 General Comments on the Country Profile

[01] The Republic of Kazakhstan (*Kazakhstan*) is located in Central Asia. Kazakhstan is the world's largest landlocked country and the ninth largest country by land area in the world (2 724.9 thousand sq. km). Kazakhstan borders Russia, China, Kyrgyzstan, Uzbekistan and Turkmenistan. It also adjoins the large part of the Caspian Sea to the east. There are fourteen oblasts and three cities of national importance: Nur-Sultan – the administrative capital of Kazakhstan, Almaty and Shymkent – the cultural, financial and economic centres of Kazakhstan. The Kazakh language is the state language, whereas Russian enjoys the status of an 'official' language and is used in official communications on an equal basis and is considered as the language of business in Kazakhstan. Kazakhstan Tenge (KZT) is the official currency and was first introduced shortly after independence in November 1993.

[02] The population of Kazakhstan is approximately 19 million people (2021) and is very ethnically diverse. There are more than a hundred ethnic groups living in Kazakhstan, with Kazakh and Russians being the most represented (approximately 69% and 19%, respectively). Uzbeks (3.29%), Ukrainians (1.36%), Uyghurs (1.48%) and Tatars (1.06%) are also significant minorities. The population has experienced steady growth since independence. Approximately 9.2 million out of 19 million constitute the economically active workforce. Kazakhstan has one of the highest literacy rates in the world (99.8% literacy).

[03] Kazakhstan has world-class hydrocarbon and mineral resources. Proven reserves of oil and natural gas are ranked 11th in the world and have been the driving force of the economy since independence. Tengiz and Kashagan are the largest oil fields in the country, whereas the Karachaganak gas deposit in the west of the country has substantial gas production. There are also around 160 smaller hydrocarbon deposits in the country, located primarily in the west of Kazakhstan. It is also estimated that Kazakhstan is the world's largest producer of uranium, zinc and lead reserves, and has abundant coal, gold, copper and other metals.

[04] Kazakhstan has a developed railroad infrastructure the total length of which is 16 634.8 km. The railroad systems of Russia and Kazakhstan are interlinked. There are around sixteen division points with Russia, China, Kyrgyzstan and Uzbekistan.

[05] There are five international autoroutes across Kazakhstan with a total length of approximately 23 000 km. Kazakhstan finished its part of the construction of a major motorway under the 'Western Europe – Western China' motorway project with a total length of 8 445 km.

[06] Due to the size of Kazakhstan's territory, air transport plays a major role in transportation. There are twenty airports, twelve of which service international flights.

1.2 Government and Political System

[07] Kazakhstan has stable relations with its neighbours and has become the most developed country in Central Asia. Kazakhstan is a member of numerous multilateral organizations, including the United Nations (UN), Organisation of Islamic Cooperation (OIC), Shanghai Cooperation Organisation (SCO), Euro-Atlantic Partnership Council (EAPC), Commonwealth of Independent States (CIS), Collective Security Treaty Organisation (CSTO) and the Organisation for Security and Cooperation in Europe (OSCE). In May 2014, Kazakhstan signed an agreement on accession to the Eurasian Economic Union with Russia and Belarus and now is part of a common economic zone which allows goods to transit freely between the Member States without any customs duties and citizens of one country to travel, live and work in the others. On 27 July 2015, Kazakhstan signed the protocol on accession to the World Trade Organization (WTO). Following successful ratification of the accession by Kazakhstan's Parliament, Kazakhstan became a full-fledged member of the WTO on 30 November 2015.

[08] In 2000, Kazakhstan became the first former republic of the Union of Soviet Socialist Republics (USSR) to repay its debt to the International Monetary Fund (IMF). In 2002, Kazakhstan received 'market economy status' under the United States (US) trade law which evidences substantial reforms in relation to openness to foreign investment, currency convertibility, wage determination and other issues.

[09] Kazakhstan has good international rankings for ease of doing business. The 2020 World Bank Report ranks Kazakhstan 25th out of 190 jurisdictions for ease of doing business. Specifically, it is ranked 22nd for starting a business, 4th for the enforcement of contracts, 64th for paying taxes and 7th for protecting minority investors. A wide network of bilateral investment treaties with over forty jurisdictions also contributes to the favourable investment climate. Notable jurisdictions include the United Kingdom (UK), US, most European countries, China, former USSR countries and certain Gulf and Asian states. On a national level, the Entrepreneurial Code sets out guarantees for investors, such as 'fair and equitable treatment', 'full protection and security', currency convertibility, transparency and a prohibition on expropriation without compensation.

1.3 Legal System

[10] Kazakhstan's legal system is based on civil law.

[11] The current Kazakhstan civil law has many similar characteristics with the law of Russia and other CIS countries due to various factors, such as (i) unified heritage of the USSR's legal system, (ii) joint elaboration of legislation in sectors of mutual interest (trade, transportation, state security, etc.), (iii) similarity of problems that CIS countries face in economic and political areas, etc.

[12] In the 2019 World Bank Report, Kazakhstan is ranked 4th out of 190 countries for ease of enforcing contracts. Its ranking is higher than for all the CIS countries. It takes approximately 370 days on average (counted from the moment when a plaintiff files a lawsuit in court until payment) to resolve a dispute.

[13] Identifying acquisition targets may not be easy. Potential investors can seek assistance from either local or international advisory organizations (such as international and local audit firms and law firms as well as investment banks/advisors) which may provide guidance in identifying acquisition targets, assist in investigating the targets and advise on any acquisition transaction. According to the Legal 500 directory, there are twenty-three law firms based in Kazakhstan and all 'Big 4' audit companies are present as well.

1.4 Current Economic Aspects

[14] The estimated growth in the gross domestic product (GDP) for 2021 is 3.2–3.7%, and it is forecasted to reach 3.7% in 2022.

[15] Currently, industrial output for the half-year amounted to approximately KZT11.8tn or approximately USD30.8bn, and gross agricultural output amounted to approximately KZT1.1tn or approximately USD2.9bn.

1.5 Main Industries

[16] The key industries of the Kazakhstan economy are: oil and gas, mining, banking, telecommunications, power and infrastructure and construction.

[17] Below are examples of M&A transactions in which our team was involved.

1.6 Oil & Gas, Mining

[18]

- MOL HUNGARIAN OIL AND GAS PLC on its sale of a 49% share in Karpovskiy Severniy LLP, a subsoil use right holder under the contract for the exploration of oil, gas and condensate at Karpovskiy Severniy contract area in Western Kazakhstan.
- INTERNATIONAL MINERAL RESOURCES II BV on the sale of 100% of issued and placed shares of KoZhaN JSC, an oil company, via open trades on the Kazakhstan Stock Exchange.

1.6.1 Banking

[19]

- – JSC HALYK BANK KAZAKHSTAN on the acquisition of a majority stake in Kazkommertsbank JSC from its controlling shareholder Mr Kenges Rakishev and National Wealth Fund Samruk-Kazyna JSC.
- – JSC HALYK BANK KAZAKHSTAN on the potential sale of a 60% stake in its subsidiary bank Altyn Bank JSC to China CITIC Bank Corporation Limited and China Shuangwei Investment Co., Ltd.
- – MR KENGES RAKISHEV on the acquisition of Alnair Capital Holding JSC and its 28.08% shareholding in Kazkommertsbank JSC, the largest bank in Kazakhstan, as a result of which Mr Rakishev increased his total shareholding in Kazkommertsbank JSC to 56.75% of its issued common share capital.

1.6.2 Telecommunications

[20]

- – TELE2 SVERIGE AB on its joint venture with Kazakhtelecom JSC, the national telecoms operator, and the combination of the cellular operations of their subsidiaries Altel JSC and Mobile Telecom-Services LLP (Tele2 Kazakhstan).

1.6.3 Infrastructure

[21]

- – A CONFIDENTIAL CLIENT on the aborted acquisition of majority shareholding in Almaty International Airport JSC.
- – A CONFIDENTIAL CLIENT on the acquisition of companies owning logistics complexes in the Russian Federation.

[22] Generally, Kazakhstan legislation does not distinguish between foreign and domestic investors and both types of investors have equal rights and protection under the law. In addition, foreign citizens have the same rights and obligations as Kazakhstan nationals unless otherwise provided by the Constitution, international treaties and legislative acts.

[23] There are, however, restrictions on the percentage of foreign ownership in certain industries. Notably, there are limits on foreign ownership in telecommunications and mass media. We note, however, that with Kazakhstan's accession to the WTO, some of these restrictions will be lifted in the next few years.

[24] There are also limitations on the transfer of ownership and establishment of encumbrances in respect of strategic assets/objects (main railway networks, main pipelines, the national electrical grid, main communication lines, television and radio broadcasting objects, etc.).

[25] Acquisitions by foreign investors usually involve strategic acquirers while local acquirers represent a mix of financial and strategic acquirers.

1.6.4 Cultural Aspects

[26] Kazakhstan is generally open and welcoming to foreign investment and a favourable place to do business. At the same time, as in any other country, there are a number of obstacles for investors to conduct their business activity. The Kazakhstan Government has, however, been working to improve the investment climate for investors.

[27] In general, most business in Kazakhstan is concentrated in two cities – Almaty and Nur-Sultan, although the oil fields are located mostly in Western Kazakhstan. Almaty, being the former capital of Kazakhstan is a financial and cultural centre, and is still the largest city in Kazakhstan. Nur-Sultan is a rapidly developing city with its recently constructed modern administrative buildings, business and entertainment centres. The cost of living in Nur-Sultan is probably equal to or greater than the cost in Almaty. Nur-Sultan successfully hosted the International Exposition (EXPO) on the theme 'Future Energy' which took place from 10 June 2017 to 10 September 2017. The Astana International Financial Centre (AIFC), aimed at establishing a leading international centre for financial services, officially launched on 5 July 2018. The AIFC operates on the basis of the EXPO-2017 infrastructure.

[28] Kazakhstan is a secular state and adheres to established international business customs. It is normal, for example, to bring a gift for the hostess when visiting a Kazakhstan home. Also, a small business gift may be appropriate, but its value should correspond to the rank of the Kazakhstan businessperson with whom one is meeting. As to state officials, giving gifts to state officials is not allowed under the law and may entail administrative or, in some cases, criminal liability. In general, normal western customs apply to Kazakhstan's business environment.

2 THE REGULATORY FRAMEWORK

2.1 Business Vehicles

[29] The most common forms of business vehicle used in Kazakhstan are the limited liability partnership (LLP) and the joint-stock company (JSC). Both an LLP and JSC are considered to be legal entities (i.e., they are deemed to have a distinct legal personality). Both the LLP and the JSC have features which are similar to those of a 'limited liability company' and of a 'company limited by shares' (or 'corporation' in the US), respectively. There are other forms of legal entities recognized in Kazakhstan (such as a partnership with unlimited liability and a limited partnership), though they are rarely used. Another form of business vehicle which is occasionally used in the business context is an 'ordinary (or simple) partnership' (also known as a 'consortium' when it is created between legal entities); however, it is not considered to be a legal entity under Kazakhstan law and, therefore, is mostly

used for specific purposes, such as in order to jointly participate in a tender. Kazakhstan law also permits foreign companies to conduct business through branches established in Kazakhstan and this option is often used. After the creation of the AIFC back in 2018, the incorporation of private companies (analogous to an LLP) becomes an option for certain businesses in Kazakhstan. A private company is a legal entity which has a separate legal personality from that of its shareholders. Though AIFC is located in Kazakhstan, it effectively has a 'separate jurisdiction' which is based on the principles of common law (i.e., the laws of England and Wales and other common law jurisdictions) and has an independent judicial system. AIFC is mainly a platform for financial services and digital assets (cryptocurrencies). It also provides a 'sand-bo' for some IT start-ups and projects (which enables to incorporate an entity in the AIFC in a simplified form).

2.2 LLP and JSC

[30] LLPs are the most common form of legal entities used and have minimal requirements. JSCs are typically used where the law specifically requires a legal entity to be established as a JSC (i.e., in regulated industries, such as banking, insurance, etc.) or for companies that wish to be publicly listed.

[31] The following table gives an overview of the main features of an LLP and JSC.

LLP	JSC
Charter capital is divided into interests held by participants (individuals and/or legal entities).	Charter capital is divided into shares held by shareholders (individuals and/or legal entities). JSC can issue common and preferred shares. Preferred shares have no voting rights (except for matters which can limit the rights of shareholders holding preferred shares) but entitle its holder to a minimum guaranteed dividend. Shares are issued in non-documentary form only.
Liability of participants is limited to the value of their respective contributions in the charter capital.	Liability of shareholders is limited to the value of their respective investments in shares.
Interests are generally reflected in the foundation agreement but a participants' register can be maintained by a central depository (currently, Central Securities Depository JSC) (the *Central Depository*).	Shareholders' register must be maintained by the Central Depository.

LLP	JSC
Minimum charter capital requirement for the medium-sized business is 100 monthly calculation indexes (MCI) (currently KZT291 700 or approximately USD678).	Minimum charter capital requirement is 50 000 MCI (currently KZT145 850 000 or approximately USD339 186).
Contributions in kind are permitted. If the value of such contributions exceeds 20 000 MCI (currently KZT58 340 000 or approximately USD135 674), its value must be verified by an independent appraiser.	Contributions in kind are made at a price determined by an independent appraiser. Contributions in kind are prohibited for certain types of JSCs, which are regulated entities (including, notably, in the financial sector).
Charter capital increases require approval by a qualified majority of votes equal to three-fourths of the votes of participants present at the meeting of participants at which at least two-thirds of the total number of votes are present (unless a higher vote is provided in the charter).	Charter capital increases are possible by way of an issue of authorized shares. An issuance of authorized shares must be approved by the board of directors. Increases in the total number of authorized shares must be approved by the shareholders.
The charter is the constitutive document.	The charter is the only constitutive document. Optionally, a corporate governance code can be adopted by the shareholders but is required for listed JSCs.
Foundation agreement is required where there are two or more participants. Foundation agreement must be governed by Kazakhstan law. The foundation agreement terminates from the moment when the participants' register is maintained by the Central Depository.	A foundation agreement is used when establishing a JSC but terminates upon the placement of the shares.
The participants have a statutory pre-emptive right to purchase the participating interests of other participants when offered for sale to third parties.	There is no pre-emptive right to purchase shares sold by existing shareholders.

LLP	JSC
Management structure includes the general meeting of participants (the supreme body) and an executive body, which usually exists in the form of a general director or a collective body such as a management board. Optionally, an LLP may have a supervisory council, which has the authority to supervise the executive body and can be roughly equivalent to a board of directors.	Management structure includes the general meeting of shareholders (the supreme body), a board of directors (the management body) and an executive body, which may be a sole executive, i.e., a general director (chief executive officer (CEO)) but usually exists in the form of a collective executive body (a management board), which is headed by its chairman.
The head of the executive body is considered to be the general director (i.e., CEO) of the company and has the sole authority to represent the company before third parties. No other person (not even a member of the supervisory council) can bind the company without a power of attorney from the CEO.	The head of the executive body is considered to be the CEO of the company and has the sole authority to represent the company before third parties. No other person (not even a director) can bind the company without a power of attorney from the CEO.
Controlling body, such as an audit committee or a sole auditor, can be created by the participants.	An internal audit committee can be created as a controlling body over financial and economic affairs of the company.
No specific supervisory authority.	The National Bank of the Republic of Kazakhstan (NBK) supervises the process of issuance, placement and circulation of shares.
No prospectus requirement.	An emission prospectus (i.e., a regulatory document setting out terms of securities) is required to be prepared in connection with the issuance of shares. The prospectus must be registered with the NBK. Certain events require the amendment of the prospectus, which must be registered with the NBK.

LLP	JSC
General meeting of participants approves annual financial statements and distribution of net proceeds. In case an LLP creates an audit committee or appoints an auditor, annual financial statements must be reviewed by it before approval by the general meeting of participants. Companies of public interest such as, for example, subsurface users or state-owned companies must publish their annual financial statements. Within two months after decreasing its charter capital an LLP must either make a public announcement or notify its creditors.	A JSC must audit its annual financial statements and must publish its annual balance sheet, profit and loss account and cash flow report.
No filing requirements, except for filings with the Ministry of Justice in case of an increase or decrease of charter capital, change of legal address, etc.	Certain information such as annual financial statements, auditors reports and corporate events must be filed with the Depositary of Financial Information. Such information is publicly available on the website of the depositary.

2.3 Simple Partnership

[32] A simple partnership (*Consortium*) is not deemed to be a legal entity. A Consortium is often used in the context where legal entities must combine their resources on a temporary basis in order to carry out a specific task. A Consortium is established by way of entering into an agreement in writing (known as an 'agreement on joint activity'). Because a Consortium is not a legal entity, it is a tax-transparent structure (i.e., the Consortium itself is not taxed and instead each of its members is taxed separately). Any property which is contributed to the Consortium by its members becomes the joint property of the Consortium. All Consortium members are jointly liable to third parties in respect of the Consortium's activity unless the agreement on joint activity provides otherwise.

2.4 Branch

[33] Kazakhstan law generally permits legal entities, including foreign legal entities, to establish branches in Kazakhstan. A branch is permitted to conduct any and all types of activities of a legal entity. Branches of foreign entities are prohibited from operating in certain sectors (such as in the financial sector). However, in connection with Kazakhstan's accession to the WTO, foreign insurance companies and foreign banks are allowed to establish their branches in Kazakhstan provided they meet certain legislative requirements. Further, local content requirements – which apply to the procurement of goods, works and services by subsurface users in Kazakhstan and by state-owned entities – limit the use of branches in certain areas because only legal entities qualify as local providers of services or goods.

2.5 Executive Authority

[34] Executive authority is vested in the head of the executive body of a legal entity. In the context of an LLP, it is the general director or, if the executive body of an LLP exists in the form of a collective executive body, it is the head (chairman) of such collective executive body. In the context of a JSC, it is usually the chairman of the management board. The head of the executive body of a legal entity can delegate his authority to another person on the basis of a power of attorney. The head of a branch exercises its executive authority on the basis of a power of attorney issued to it by the legal entity that established the branch.

2.6 Laws Affecting M&A

[35] The main laws involved in M&A activity in Kazakhstan are the Civil Code[1] and, depending on the type of company that is being acquired, either the LLP Law[2] or the JSC Law[3] and the Securities Law.[4] In addition, the Economic Competition Section of the Entrepreneurial Code has a significant impact on M&A activity in Kazakhstan. Finally, other laws may apply depending on the industry within which the target business operates.

[36] Kazakhstan law does not distinguish between private and public deals. The main difference between deals involving LLPs and JSCs is that where the target is a

---

[1] Collectively, the Civil Code (General Part) of the Republic of Kazakhstan dated 27 Dec. 1994 and the Civil Code (Special Part) of the Republic of Kazakhstan No. 409-I dated 1 Jul. 1999, as amended (the *Civil Code*).

[2] Law of the Republic of Kazakhstan 'On Limited and Additional Liability Partnerships' No. 220-I dated 22 Apr. 1998, as amended (the *LLP Law*).

[3] Law of the Republic of Kazakhstan 'On Joint Stock Companies' No. 415-II dated 13 May 2003, as amended (the *JSC Law*).

[4] Law of the Republic of Kazakhstan 'On the Securities Market' No. 461-II dated 2 Jul. 2003, as amended (the *Securities Law*).

JSC there may be a mandatory tender offer requirement. Similarly, Kazakhstan law does not distinguish between friendly/agreed transactions and hostile transactions. We note that hostile transactions do not really exist in Kazakhstan. Shareholders of a JSC have the right to sell their shares as they wish but there is no mechanism for an acquirer to squeeze out the minority except for the following provision under the JSC Law: an acquirer of 95 or more per cent of the voting shares of the company has a right to demand that the other remaining shareholders of the company (i.e., the minority shareholders) sell their voting shares in the company to him.

[37] The main way in which companies and businesses can combine is through the acquisition of shares in a JSC or participating interests in the charter capital of an LLP. It is the most often used and preferred M&A method. It is also possible to acquire the assets of another company. However, where a business relies on a licence, an asset acquisition may not be a viable option because under the general rule licences in Kazakhstan are non-transferrable. A reorganization of a company is possible. However, as a rule, it is not used in the context of M&A transactions.

[38] There are no voluntary codes, guidelines or self-regulation mechanisms that apply in the context of an M&A transaction.

[39] A legal entity may be reorganized in a number of ways, one of which is by way of a merger. After the merger of two entities, their rights and obligations transfer to an entity created as a result of such a merger. The transfer of rights and obligations is carried out on the basis of a transfer act. In practice, mergers do not occur very often.

2.7 Relevant Regulatory Authorities

[40] There are several governmental/regulatory authorities in Kazakhstan in the context of an M&A transaction. The Agency for Protection and Development of Competition of the Republic of Kazakhstan (the *Antimonopoly Agency*) is responsible for granting antimonopoly clearances for proposed M&A transactions and for issuing consents and receiving notifications in respect of an acquisition of shares in, and assets of, legal entities. The NBK is the relevant government authority for the purposes of exchange control and securities laws. The Ministry of Justice of the Republic of Kazakhstan (the *Ministry of Justice*) is responsible for registering legal entities in Kazakhstan and also for registering any changes to the participants of LLPs unless a register of participants is maintained by the Central Depository.

[41] There are a number of government authorities that grant consent for proposed M&A transactions. For instance, the Ministry of Energy of the Republic of Kazakhstan (the MoE) and the Ministry of Industry and Infrastructure Development of the Republic of Kazakhstan (the MIID) (depending on the type of mineral) are the relevant government authorities for issuing consents for alienation of shares/participating interests in subsurface users and subsurface use rights. Under

the new Subsurface Code,[5] the consent of local Akimats for alienation of shares/participating interests in subsurface users and subsurface use rights related to commonly occurring minerals is not required. However, because the Subsurface Code is a relatively new act, this particular matter is untested and consent may in practice be required. At the beginning of 2019, certain ministries and their committees were reorganized. The regulations of the relevant ministries and committees do not set out all of their competencies. Therefore, there is currently some uncertainty as to which ministry or committee is responsible for issuing consents for the acquisition of shares of intercity or international telecommunications providers. Under the law, an authorized body in the field of communication and information is responsible for issuing consents for the acquisition of shares of telecommunications providers. Based on its name, we believe that currently the Committee of Telecommunications of the Ministry of Digital Development, Defence and Aerospace Industry of the Republic of Kazakhstan (the *Communications Authority*) is the relevant government authority for issuing consents for the acquisition of shares of telecommunications providers. Finally, the Kazakhstan Government is the relevant government authority for issuing consents for alienation of shares and assets deemed to constitute 'strategic assets/objects'.

[42] Under the legislation, depending on the type of consent, it takes from twenty to sixty business days to obtain consent. In practice, however, this may take longer. A legal entity, be it a local or a foreign legal entity, interested in obtaining the relevant consents can independently apply for such consent. However, due to the vast experience of advisors in these types of applications, legal entities tend to hire a professional advisor to assist them in preparing and submitting the applications required to obtain consent.

2.8 Controls/Restrictions on Foreign Investment

[43] Kazakhstan law provides restrictions on foreign ownership in certain types of industries. There is a restriction on maximum foreign ownership, which is limited to certain industries deemed to have particular importance for national security. Other restrictions are mostly indirect and technically apply to both domestic and foreign acquirers. However, in practice, the state has occasionally used some of these restrictions in order to exercise control over foreign investment in certain industries. One of the notable examples of such restriction is the state's pre-emptive right to acquire shares or assets in certain industries. Other notable restrictions are mostly in the form of a requirement to obtain prior approval to make an investment in a certain industry.

---

[5] The Subsurface and Subsurface Use Code of the Republic of Kazakhstan dated 27 Dec. 2017 No. 125-VI, as amended (the *Subsurface Code*).

2.9 Maximum Limits on Foreign Ownership

[44] The key restrictions on foreign ownership exist in the telecommunications and mass media sectors. These restrictions are established pursuant to the National Security Law.[6]

[45] In the telecommunications sector, foreign nationals and foreign legal entities are not allowed to possess, use, dispose of and/or manage, directly or indirectly, in aggregate more than 49% of the voting shares (interests) in a legal entity, which conducts activity in the area of telecommunications as an intercity and/or an international operator, and which owns landline (cable, including fibre optic, radio relay) facilities without the prior positive consent of the Government of the Republic of Kazakhstan.

[46] In the mass media sector, foreign individuals and foreign legal entities are not allowed to possess, use, dispose of and/or manage, directly or indirectly, more than 20% of shares (interests) in a legal entity, which is the owner of mass media in Kazakhstan or which conducts its activity in this area.

[47] Because the restrictions apply to indirect ownership, the above restrictions cannot be circumvented by acquisition through a locally formed special purpose vehicle (SPV) which is owned by foreign interests.

[48] In addition, in case of the acquisition of more than 10% of the voting shares (interests) in an entity, which owns and/or conducts activities as an intercity or an international telecommunications operator or that owns telecommunications lines, any investor that intends to acquire such shares (interests) is required to receive the consent of the Communications Authority and the Committee of National Security of the Republic of Kazakhstan. The Communications Authority must consider such application within thirty days of its receipt. However, in practice, the consideration process may take a longer period of time (two to three months).

[49] In addition, due to recent legislative amendments to the Aviation Law,[7] foreign nationals and foreign legal entities are not allowed to own directly and/or indirectly more than 49% of the total amount of shares in air companies established in the form of a JSC. Under the law, air companies carrying out regularly scheduled flights must be established as JSCs.

---

[6] Law of the Republic of Kazakhstan 'On National Security' No. 527-IV dated 6 Jan. 2012, as amended (the *National Security Law*).

[7] Law of the Republic of Kazakhstan 'On the Use of the Airspace of the Republic of Kazakhstan and Aviation Activities' No. 339-IV dated 15 Jul. 2010, as amended (the *Aviation Law*).

2.10 Restrictions in Respect of Land Ownership and Usage

[50] There are certain restrictions on ownership or usage of land by foreign companies or individuals. These restrictions are established in the Land Code.[8] In particular, foreign individuals, foreign companies as well as Kazakhstan companies owned by foreign individuals or foreign companies are not permitted to own agricultural land and forestry land.

2.11 State's Pre-emptive Right in Respect of Assets Designated as 'Strategic Objects'

[51] The Civil Code provides that the sale and encumbrance of strategic objects are possible only on the basis of a decision of the Kazakhstan Government to provide its consent. This procedure is established by the State Property Law.[9]

[52] The State Property Law defines 'strategic objects' as property which has a social and an economic significance for the stable development of Kazakhstan society and the ownership, possession and (or) disposal of which may affect the national security of Kazakhstan. The list of strategic objects may include such assets as main communications lines, international airports, the national postal network, shareholdings in legal entities that own strategic objects, shareholdings in legal entities that may directly or indirectly determine decisions or influence the decisions of legal entities that own strategic objects, etc. The precise list of strategic objects is approved by the Kazakhstan Government. The most recent version of the list was approved by the Kazakhstan Government on 30 June 2008, as amended.

[53] Government consent for the disposal of strategic assets should normally be given or refused within forty-five business days following the date of receipt of the relevant documents by the authorized body in the relevant sphere. However, in practice consideration of the application may take longer (three to six months).

2.12 State's Pre-emptive Right in Respect of Subsurface Use Rights

[54] The Subsurface Code requires that the consent of the competent authority be obtained prior to the alienation of subsurface use rights or so-called objects related to subsurface use rights (meaning an interest (share) in a company having subsurface use rights or an interest (share) in a company (even a foreign company) which

---

8 Land Code of the Republic of Kazakhstan No. 442-II dated 20 Jun. 2003, as amended (the *Land Code*).

9 Law of the Republic of Kazakhstan 'On State Property' No. 413-IV dated 1 Mar. 2011, as amended (the *State Property Law*).

directly or indirectly holds interests in a subsurface user). In addition to the consent of the competent authority, waiver of the state's priority right of purchase is required with respect to certain strategic deposits/objects related to subsurface use rights. Strategic deposits are established by a list approved by a resolution of the Kazakhstan Government. In order to obtain such waiver and consent, the acquirer must file an application with the competent authority containing, among other things, information about the acquirer and its participants (with an indication of the participating interests/shares held). Application for the waiver/consent should be made prior to the transaction.

[55] Further, notification should be given to the competent authority of all transactions with objects related to subsurface use rights. Notification should be made within one month upon completion of the transaction.

[56] The competent authority is the MIID for mineral subsurface use contracts, the MoE for hydrocarbon contracts and the Akimats for common minerals. The Subsurface Code provides for a period of one month to three months (depending on the deposit) to obtain the consent. In practice, this can take longer. The competent authority's consent is valid for a period of one year after it is issued.

[57] Certain exemptions are available. For example, trading in shares and/or other securities do not require waiver/consent/notification if such shares/securities circulate on the organized securities market. A case-by-case analysis is necessary to advise whether a particular share/security may be viewed as 'circulating on the organized securities market'.

[58] A transaction performed without the required consent is null and void. Furthermore, failure to obtain such waiver and/or consent can provide the basis for the authorities to terminate the underlying subsurface use rights.

2.13 Blacklisted Jurisdictions

[59] Kazakhstan law establishes a list of blacklisted jurisdictions for the purposes of ownership of shares in banks and certain other types of financial institutions. Legal entities registered in offshore zones, the list of which is determined by an authorized body, may not possess, use or dispose of, directly or indirectly, any voting shares of Kazakhstan banks and Kazakhstan insurance organizations. In addition, the acquisition of voting shares of Kazakhstan banks and certain other types of financial institutions by an entity that has affiliated entities established in a blacklisted jurisdiction is prohibited. There is an exception to this prohibition for non-resident banks and non-resident insurance organizations with a minimum required rating assigned by one of the rating agencies (e.g., A-rated foreign banks). The list of the rating agencies and the minimum required rating are determined by an authorized body. The authorized body is the NBK.

[60] The following blacklisted jurisdictions are currently included in the NBK's list: (USA) (in respect of the following territories only: The Virgin Islands of the (US), Wyoming, Guam, Delaware, Commonwealth of Puerto Rico), Principality of

Andorra, Antigua and Barbuda, Commonwealth of The Bahamas, Barbados, Belize, Negara Brunei Darussalam, United Republic of Tanzania, Republic of Vanuatu, Republic of Guatemala, Grenada, Republic of Djibouti, Commonwealth of Dominica, Dominican Republic, Kingdom of Spain (in respect of the territories of the Canary Islands only), Federal Islamic Republic of the Comoros, Co-operative Republic of Guyana, Republic of Cyprus; People's Republic of China (in respect of the territories of the special administrative regions of Aomin (Macau) only), Republic of Costa Rica, Republic of Liberia, Lebanese Republic, Principality of Liechtenstein, Islamic Republic of Mauritania, Malaysia (in respect of the territory of Labuan enclave only), Republic of Mauritius, Republic of Maldives, Mariana Islands, Republic of the Marshall Islands, Principality of Monaco, Republic of Malta, Union of Myanmar, Republic of Nauru, Kingdom of the Netherlands (in respect of the territories of the islands of Aruba and dependent territories of the Antilles islands only), Federal Republic of Nigeria, New Zealand (in respect of the territories of the Cook Islands and Niue only), Republic of Palau, Republic of Panamá, Portugal (only in part of the territory of the Madeira Islands); Independent State of Samoa, Republic of Seychelles, Saint Vincent and the Grenadines, Saint Kitts and Nevis, Saint Lucia, the Republic of Suriname, Kingdom of Tonga, The Republic of Trinidad and Tobago, (UK) of Great Britain and Northern Ireland (in respect of the following territories only: Anguilla, Bermuda, the British Virgin Islands, Gibraltar, the Cayman Islands, Montserrat, the Turks and Caicos Islands, Islands of Normandy (Sark and Alderney), Island of South Georgia, South Sandwich Islands, Chagos Island), Sovereign Democratic Republic of Fiji, Republic of the Philippines, French Republic (only in respect of the following territories: Kerguelen Islands; French Guiana; French Polynesia); Republic of Montenegro, Democratic Socialist Republic of Sri Lanka, Jamaica.

2.14 Local Partner, Permit to Trade, Etc.

[61] There is no permit to trade required for a foreign-owned company. Additionally, there are no minimum capital requirements or capital import requirements established for foreign companies owning Kazakhstan entities. Foreign-owned Kazakhstan companies are subject to the same requirements as any Kazakhstan legal entity.

2.15 Incentives for Foreign Investment

[62] Generally, issues related to investment in Kazakhstan are regulated by the Entrepreneurial Code, the Tax Code[10] and the SEIZ Law.[11]

---

[10] The Code of the Republic of Kazakhstan 'On Taxes and Other Obligatory Payments to the Budget' (Tax Code) No. 120-VI dated 25 Dec. 2017, as amended (the *Tax Code*).
[11] Law of the Republic of Kazakhstan 'On Special Economic Zones and Industrial Zones' No. 242-VI dated 3 Apr. 2019 (the *SEIZ Law*).

In addition to the above, on 5 July 2018, a financial centre, the AIFC, was established in order to attract foreign investment to Kazakhstan. AIFC operates within a special legal regime based on English Law and provides its members with a preferential tax regime, simplified currency control, beneficial visa and employment regimes, simplified registration processes and services of its own independent financial and arbitration courts.

2.16 Entrepreneurial Code

[63] The Entrepreneurial Code, which applies to both foreign and domestic investors, regulates investment relationships in Kazakhstan. In particular, it sets forth the basic principles of investment protection and it provides for the 'investment project', 'priority investment project' and 'special investment project' regimes.

[64] 'Investment project' means a set of measures which envisages investment in the formation of new production facilities, or the development and/or modernization of existing production facilities, including production facilities formed, developed and/or modernized through the implementation of public and private partnership projects, including by a concessionaire (legal successor) within the framework of a concession agreement.

[65] 'Priority investment project' means an investment project (a) on the formation of new production facilities, which provides for investment by a legal entity into the construction of new production facilities (factory, plant, workshop) in an amount not less than approximately USD13.6m; (b) on the development and/or modernization of existing production facilities which provides for investments by a legal entity in an amount of not less than approximately USD34m for the modification of fixed assets, including renewal (renovation, reconstruction, modernization) of existing production facilities that produce goods/products.

'Priority investment project' is implemented by a legal entity in accordance with certain priority types of activity, the list of which is approved by the Kazakhstan Government, and which includes, *inter alia*, plant raising and animal breeding; production of food or machines; production of coke, refined petroleum products; production of goods in the iron and steel industry, etc.

[66] 'Special investment project' means: (a) an investment project which has been implemented and/or is being implemented by a Kazakhstan legal entity which is registered as: (i) a participant of a special economic zone (SEZ); or (ii) as an owner of a free warehouse in accordance with the customs legislation of Kazakhstan; and/or (b) a project obtained from the participant of a SEZ or implemented by a Kazakhstan legal entity which has executed an agreement on industrial assembly of motor vehicles.

[67] Investment preferences under the Investment Law are granted through the execution of an investment contract with a Kazakhstan legal entity (including those owned by a foreign company) that implements an investment project.

[68] The Entrepreneurial Code provides for the following investment preferences through the execution of an investment contract:

(a) relief from customs duties on import of certain types of equipment, spare parts and raw materials;
(b) state grants in the form of land plots, industrial buildings and equipment for use by investors;
(c) relief from land and property tax;
(d) relief from corporate income tax (CIT) and value added tax (VAT);
(e) investment subsidies.

[69] Investors may enjoy the following investment preferences:

Under 'investment projects'

(a) relief from import customs duties and VAT;
(b) state grants.

Under 'priority investment projects'

(a) 100% decrease of sums of assessed CIT;
(b) nil rate for land tax;
(c) nil rate for property tax;
(d) investment subsidies.

Under 'special investment projects'

(a) relief from import customs duties.

2.17 Guarantees and Protections Provided by the Entrepreneurial Code

[70] Legal entities which implement 'priority investment projects' and 'strategic investment projects' under investment contracts entered into prior to 1 January 2015, or 'investment projects' in the framework of an investment agreement will have the following guarantees:

(a) tax stability; and
(b) guarantees relating to the attraction of foreign labour.

[71] The guarantees will be annulled in the event of early termination of the investment contract.

[72] The Entrepreneurial Code contains a number of provisions that provide protection to investors. It includes provisions governing dispute resolution and contract stability, protection against illegal acts of state bodies, the right for compensation of damages incurred by an investor due to the illegal acts of state bodies, the right to use and dispose of revenues and protection against nationalization and expropriation. The Entrepreneurial Code introduced a principle of 'one window', where the communication with investors is limited to one party – National Company "KAZAKH INVEST" JSC. At the state level protection of investors is carried out by the investment ombudsman.

[73] Investors are guaranteed the right to use their income (including income on payment of interest on foreign loans or payment of fees and charges to foreign companies for intellectual property (IP) or technology transfer) at their own discretion after the payment of taxes and other obligatory payments. The guarantee to use after-tax income is subject to Kazakhstan currency laws, which for foreign investors allow proceeds to be freely repatriated.

2.18 Investment Preferences under Currency Laws

[74] Generally, the foreign currency regulations in Kazakhstan are not overly restrictive and are less restrictive for non-residents than residents. However, under the Currency Law,[12] branches or representative offices of foreign non-financial organizations who are recognized as permanent establishment (PE) under the Tax Code are classified as residents of Kazakhstan. Such status entails the need to carry out payment with other residents of Kazakhstan in national currency. Certain exceptions though apply, notably, currency operations between branches (representative offices) of foreign legal entities.

It is permissible for a local/domestic company to maintain offshore bank accounts provided that such local company notifies the NBK about opening such offshore bank accounts and files quarterly reports on the operations with such accounts.

[75] Both residents and non-residents may buy and sell foreign currency in the internal currency market with certain limitations. Such limitations generally provide that resident legal entities (except for authorized banks) may buy non-cash foreign currency in an amount not exceeding USD50 000 per day. The Kazakhstan currency laws also require resident legal entities to indicate the purpose of buying foreign currency.

[76] Financing from banks and other third parties in the form of a loan is one of the financing options for acquisition in Kazakhstan. Some domestic banks in Kazakhstan undertake to lend for large-scale investments. Where financing is provided by foreign banks, generally, it is permissible for a foreign lender to take security over local movable and immovable property.

---

[12] Law of the Republic of Kazakhstan 'On Currency Regulation and Currency Control' No. 167-VI dated 2 Jul. 2018, as amended, (the *Currency Law*).

2.19 Investment Preferences for Special Economic and Industrial Zones

[77] Establishment and operation of special economic zones (SEZs) and industrial zones (IZs) (collectively, SEIZ) in Kazakhstan as well as investment incentives for participants of SEIZ are generally regulated by the SEIZ Law and the Tax Code.

[78] SEZ are the areas with a special legal framework for the implementation of priority types of activities.

[79] Under the SEIZ Law, legal entities (including foreign companies and Kazakhstan companies owned by foreign shareholders/participants) may apply to create an SEZ by submitting a 'concept' to the authorized body. Upon receipt of a concept, the authorized body checks the concept for compliance with the requirements for concepts of creating an SEZ. According to the results of the verification of the concept, the authorized body either submits the concept for consideration by the expert council or provides its reasoned refusal in the event the concept does not comply with the established requirements.

If the expert council issues a positive opinion, the authorized body develops and submits for consideration by the Government of the Republic of Kazakhstan a draft resolution of the Kazakhstan Government on the establishment of an SEZ and an expert opinion.

[80] The applicants for the creation of an SEZ must have sufficient funding and their proposal must fit the types of activities intended to be performed in the SEZ. The following entities cannot apply for the establishment of an SEZ:

(a) subsurface users;
(b) manufacturers of excisable goods, with some exceptions;
(c) entities that already enjoy tax relief under a special tax regime;
(d) entities that enjoy investment tax preferences under investment contracts entered into before 1 January 2009;
(e) entities implementing (which have implemented) investment priority and strategic investment projects; and
(f) entities engaged in gambling.

[81] IZs are the areas which are equipped with engineering and communication infrastructure to be provided to legal entities for placement and exploitation of the objects of entrepreneurial activity, including the production sector, agricultural complex, the tourist industry, transportation logistics and waste management. Further, IZs are divided into:

(i) governmental zones (classified by (a) IZ of republican importance, (b) IZ of regional importance, and (c) small IZ); and
(ii) private IZ.

'IZ of republican importance' is recognized if (i) it will be financed (in full or partially) from the republican budget, or (ii) it obtained its status of IZ after the abolition of an SEZ.

'IZ of regional importance' is recognized if it will be financed (in full or partially) from the local budget.

'Small IZ' must be located within the territories containing commissioned production and other premises which are provided to entities of small- and medium-scale enterprises.

'Private IZ' is created by individuals and non-governmental legal entities who are the owners of (i) land plots, which will obtain the status of private IZ, or (ii) infrastructure assets located on land plots which will obtain the status of private IZ. Private IZs are financed by the founders at their own expense and through the attraction of private investments and loans.

Under the SEIZ Law, the IZs are created based on a concept for the creation of an IZ. The concept must contain, *inter alia*, the purpose for the creation of the IZ, an environmental assessment, scheme/programme for the proposed IZ, a plan for attracting investments in a special IZ, the protocol of intentions with a potential management company (if a non-state legal entity is involved), and participation of a special IZ in the socio-economic development of the corresponding region.

[82] The management functions over the SEZ and IZ are entrusted to a managing company, a legal entity established for these specific purposes.

Once created, both SEZ and IZ exist for up to twenty-five years with the possibility of extension.

[83] SEIZ are areas within Kazakhstan with tax, customs, land and other investment privileges provided pursuant to the SEIZ Law.

2.20 Specific Issues of Company/Securities Law
Shareholder Approval

[84] In a JSC, no shareholder approval is required to be obtained for a sale of shares of the JSC (please also *see* section '*Specific Rules on Public Takeovers*' in respect of the purchase of 30% or more of the voting shares in a JSC).

[85] In an LLP, approval of the participants in the LLP may be required because the LLP Law provides for the pre-emptive right of the participants and of the LLP itself to acquire participating interests in the LLP at the time of a sale of the participating interests to third parties. Participants of an LLP have the right in preference to third parties to purchase a participant's participating interest in case one of the participants sells its interest, except as otherwise provided for by legislation. Any of the participants may exercise such right. If there are several participants willing to exercise their pre-emptive right to purchase, the participants may (unless the foundation documents or any other agreement of participants of the LLP provide otherwise) exercise their pre-emptive right to purchase any participating interest in proportion to their interests in the charter capital of such LLP. A participant of the LLP willing to sell its participating interest to a third party is obligated to notify the executive body of the LLP of such intent, specifying the proposed sale price. If none of the participants elects to exercise their pre-emptive right to purchase any

participating interest where it is offered to a third party for sale, the LLP may itself exercise such pre-emptive right to purchase.

[86] In a JSC, either the management board/sole executive of the JSC may undertake the transaction or, if it is of a size such that it qualifies as a major transaction, then the board of directors' approval will be required. If a JSC decides to participate in the establishment or activity of other legal entities by way of a transfer of assets which in aggregate constitute 25% or more of the book value of its total assets, such transaction will require shareholders' approval.

2.20.1 Directors Duties

[87] There are no specific directors' duties owed to the company, its shareholders/participants or third parties when the company is engaged in an M&A transaction. The JSC Law establishes that officials:

(1) must perform their duties in good faith; and
(2) must use means which are in the best interest of the company and its shareholders.

[88] The officers must neither use nor permit the use of the company's property:

(1) in contravention of the company's charter or the resolutions of its general meeting of shareholders or board of directors; or
(2) for their personal advantage.

2.20.2 Form of Consideration

[89] Under the JSC Law, shares in companies other than financial institutions (banks, insurance companies, etc.) can be placed for a non-cash consideration such as assets, property rights (including rights to IP items), property use rights and other rights such as the provision of works and services.

[90] Shares in financial institutions can be placed in exchange for cash only. This requirement does not apply to banks in cases where:

(1) shares in a bank are placed to creditors of the bank and are paid for by way of set-off of any right of claim in respect of any monetary liability of the bank to its respective creditor, where the bank conducts restructuring in cases provided for by the laws of the Republic of Kazakhstan;
(2) bank's securities and monetary obligations are converted into common shares of the bank in case of application of measures aimed at the workout of the insolvent bank;
(3) securities are converted into shares of a bank on the basis of the relevant prospectus for the issue of convertible securities;

(4) bank shares of one type are exchanged for shares of a bank of another type based on the charter of the bank and its share issuance prospectus;

(5) any shares in the bank are paid for in the course of a reorganization; and

(6) bank shares are paid for by government securities of the Republic of Kazakhstan.

[91] In the event that shares are placed in exchange for property other than cash (except for securities), the value of the property must be determined by a licensed Kazakhstan appraiser. The value of securities traded on a stock exchange and being transferred in payment for the placed shares in a company must be determined by way of evaluation in accordance with the methodology established by the stock exchange for the evaluation of financial instruments. Where it is impossible to evaluate such securities through such methodology, or if there is no such methodology in respect of the kind of securities which are contributed in payment for shares, their value has to be determined by a licensed Kazakhstan appraiser.

[92] There are no restrictions on the subsequent disposal of shares acquired as a result of a contribution in kind.

[93] In an LLP, a contribution to the charter capital may be in the form of cash, securities, assets, property rights, including any right to use land and any right to the results of IP rights, or other property. Contributions other than cash must be valued pursuant to an agreement of all participants or under a decision of the general meeting of participants of the LLP. If the value of such contribution exceeds the equivalent of 20 000 MCI (currently KZT58 340 000 or approximately USD135 674) its value must be determined by an independent licensed appraiser.

2.20.3 Financial Assistance

[94] Where the acquisition of shares/participating interests in a Kazakhstan company is being financed by bank loans, the banks may require security from members of the target group to guarantee loans made to the acquiring company. In general, there are no prohibitions against the granting of such security to banks. However, granting security over certain types of assets (e.g., subsurface use rights, strategic objects) will require the obtaining of consent from the relevant state authorities.

[95] Strategic assets/objects (as described in section *Controls/Restrictions on Foreign Investment* above) or shares included in the list of 'strategic assets' may only be pledged if the owner of the strategic assets/objects has obtained the written consent of the Kazakhstan Government and pledges are made in accordance with the procedure prescribed by the Kazakhstan Government.

[96] Subsurface use rights (but not the deposit to which the rights relate) may be pledged. Subsurface use rights related to hydrocarbons may be pledged, but only if the financing is for purposes connected with the development of the subsurface rights. Thus, such rights or shares may not be used to secure acquisition financing. Note that such pledges must be registered with the competent authority. Further, upon enforcement of a pledge, the sale of pledged subsurface use rights must be

carried out through a public auction and participation in the public auction requires the prior consent of the competent authority.

[97] A company can provide financial assistance for the purchase of its own shares. Depending on the company's constitutional documents, the passing of a special resolution (e.g., approval of general meeting of shareholders or participants) may be required to provide such financial assistance.

2.20.4 Security Interests

[98] Kazakhstan law recognizes the following main types of security: (i) pledge; (ii) guarantee; (iii) suretyship; (iv) penalty; (v) taking possession of the debtor's property; (vi) deposit payment and any other methods that the parties may agree to.

[99] The typical and most usual forms of security in financial transactions are the pledges and the guarantee.

[100] Pledges may be granted over most kinds of property. The basic types of the pledge are those over movable and immovable property. We note that it is possible to create a pledge over future property that is similar to a floating charge. However, as a practical matter, it is advisable periodically to amend/revise such pledge to reflect the property covered and, if registered, to register the amended/revised pledge.

[101] Depending on the type of collateral, perfection of a pledge may require registration, the government's consent (e.g., in the case of 'strategic assets/objects' as outlined above), or notification of the debtor or, in certain instances, the relevant counterparty (e.g., in the case of receivables under a contract).

[102] Registration of a pledge is required in order for the pledge to be valid where the collateral is either immovable property or movable property that is subject to mandatory state registration. A pledge agreement must also be registered if it prohibits repledge of the collateral or specifically requires registration in order to be valid even if the collateral is a type that is not subject to mandatory registration. Where registration is not required, registration is nevertheless always recommended to establish the priority of the pledgeholder over subsequently registered pledgeholders and overall unregistered pledge holders.

[103] There are no specific registration requirements in respect of guarantees for the purposes of the validity of a guarantee.

2.20.5 Enforcing a Pledge

[104] A secured party cannot automatically assume ownership of pledged property in case of default of a debtor. Generally, a pledge in Kazakhstan may only be enforced by way of either: (a) a court procedure in situations where Kazakhstan law specifically prohibits an out-of-court enforcement procedure or where the collateral is such that it requires a court-administered sale under law (e.g., subsurface use rights); or (b) an out-of-court procedure, if agreed by the parties and not prohibited by law. In both cases, a public sale (auction) of the collateral is required. Therefore, it is not easy to automatically enforce a pledge in practice. The process usually takes two months or more.

[105] A sale is not required in case of the enforcement of a pledge over monies and receivables. A pledge over this type of collateral is enforced by way of transfer of the monies which are the subject of such pledge or which are due under the pledged rights (claims). Where it is impossible to transfer monies at the time of enforcement (e.g., receivables) – then such pledge is enforced by way of transfer to the pledge-holder of the pledgor's rights to the collateral (i.e., such pledge acts more like an assignment).

[106] In the event of insolvency of the debtor, secured creditors would receive amounts due to them only after full satisfaction of claims of creditors in the first level of priority (e.g., social and pension payments, payments of alimony, etc.). Secured creditors' claims are ranked as the second priority under the Bankruptcy Law.[13] Secured creditors may receive the collateral in-kind in exchange for repayment by the secured creditor to creditors on the first level of priority.

[107] There is a risk that a transaction including the granting of security entered into by a debtor within three years prior to initiation of the bankruptcy could be recognized as invalid by a court (i) if the transaction does not comply with Kazakhstan law requirements, (ii) if the transaction was entered into under the influence of fraud, violence, or threat, or (iii) if it is a transaction concluded on extremely unprofitable conditions for one of the parties (hard bargain), or (iv) based on other grounds stipulated in Kazakhstan law.

2.20.6 Completion Formalities

[108] Except for mandatory registration with the relevant registering authority (which applies to certain types of assets), there are no particular formalities required to effect the transfer of shares, land or other assets in Kazakhstan. Title to immovable property (land, buildings) and certain types of movable property (cars, participating interests in LLPs) must be registered with the relevant state authority (depending on the type of property). Title over shares (and participating interests in LLPs where the register of participants is maintained by the Central Depository) must be registered with the Central Depository. Transfer of participating interests in LLPs not having a register of participants requires re-registration of the LLP with the Ministry of Justice to reflect the change of participants.

2.20.7 Costs and Fees

[109] Normally, the main costs, fees and expenses arising for the parties to acquisition transactions are: (i) notarization, legalization/apostillation of transaction

---

[13] Law of the Republic of Kazakhstan 'On Rehabilitation and Bankruptcy' No. 176-V dated 7 Mar. 2014, as amended (the *Bankruptcy Law*).

documents which are executed outside Kazakhstan, (ii) translation of transaction documents executed in a foreign language into the Russian and Kazakh languages, and (iii) bank fees for the transfer of monies and conversion of currency (if applicable).

[110] In general, the scope of filing, disclosure, notification and announcement requirements will depend on the type of target company and on the number of shares/participating interests which are being acquired in such target company.

[111] Under the JSC Law, shareholders who obtain an interest (the total number of voting shares in the company) of 10% or above will need to notify the company and provide information about the shareholders' affiliates within seven days after such affiliation occurs.

2.20.8 Dividends

[112] Payment of dividends in a JSC is regulated by the JSC Law. The JSC Law provides that a company may by a resolution of a simple majority of shareholders present and voting at a general meeting of shareholders declare annual dividends on the company's shares. The JSC Law also allows semi-annual or quarterly dividends to be declared on the shares provided that the charter permits such dividends and after an audit of the financial statements of the company for the relevant period has been carried out. The company may distribute dividends on the shares only if the company has net income in the relevant period.

[113] The JSC Law prohibits the payment of dividends on shares if:

(1) the company's own capital is negative or would become negative as a result of such payment; or
(2) the company demonstrates, or the payment of dividends would cause the company to demonstrate, characteristics of insolvency.

[114] The Banking Law[14] and Insurance Law[15] also provide for some specific limitations on the payment of dividends by banks and insurance companies respectively.

[115] Subject to the shareholder's written consent, the company may pay dividends in the form of shares or bonds issued by the company (but not in the form of any other type of securities).

[116] Payment of dividends to participants in an LLP is regulated by the LLP Law. The LLP Law provides that the participants in an LLP have the right to receive net income (dividends) received by the partnership upon the annual, semi-annual and

---

[14] Law of the Republic of Kazakhstan 'On Banks and Banking Activity in the Republic of Kazakhstan', No. 2444 dated 31 Aug. 1995, as amended (the *Banking Law*).
[15] Law of the Republic of Kazakhstan 'On Insurance Activity', No. 126-II dated 18 Dec. 2000, as amended (the *Insurance Law*).

quarterly results of its activities in accordance with the decision of its general meeting approving the results of the partnership (for the relevant year, half-year or three months period respectively).

[117] In the event that the general meeting of an LLP takes a decision to distribute income between participants, each participant shall have the right to receive a part of the income to be distributed corresponding to his share in the charter capital of the partnership. Payment must be performed by the partnership in the monetary form within one month from the date when the general meeting took a decision to distribute net income. In contrast to the JSC Law, the LLP Law does not explicitly provide any restrictions on an LLP distributing dividends among its participants (i.e., negative capital, etc.).

2.20.9 Purchase of Own Shares

[118] Subject to the JSC Law and the Securities Law, a JSC may purchase its own shares. Such shares will be credited to the company's account with the Central Depository.

[119] The company cannot purchase any of its shares which are being placed in a primary offering.

[120] Any purchase by the company must be effected with the consent of the relevant shareholder using a valuation methodology that has been approved in advance by the founders or shareholders. The valuation methodology does not apply to any purchase which is effected on the stock exchange using an open trade method.

[121] In certain circumstances provided for by the JSC Law, and subject to certain conditions set out in the JSC Law, the company must repurchase shares belonging to a shareholder within thirty days of receiving a duly formalized request from such shareholder.

[122] Shares being repurchased by the company cannot exceed 25% of the total number of issued/placed shares of the company, and the purchase price for such shares cannot exceed 10% of the size of the company's own capital.

[123] The proceeds from the sale of shares to the JSC can be freely repatriated.

2.20.10 The Corporate Veil

[124] It is a general principle under Kazakhstan law that a company is considered to be a separate legal entity from both its shareholders and its subsidiaries. Parent companies are not liable for the obligations of their subsidiaries. The shareholders (participants) bear the risk of loss up to the value of their shares (interests) in the company except in certain cases provided for by the Kazakhstan legislation.

[125] There is a general principle under Kazakhstan civil law which states that if a premeditated or fraudulent bankruptcy of a legal entity was caused by the actions of its founder (participant) or the owner of its property, then, in cases where the

legal entity's funds are insufficient, the founder (participant) or the owner of its property, as appropriate, bears secondary/subsidiary liability to the entity's creditors.

[126] In addition, there are the following exceptions to the limited liability of parent companies:

(1) in cases where actions of the parent company cause the bankruptcy of a subsidiary, the parent company will also be held to bear secondary/subsidiary liability for the debts of the subsidiary; and

(2) the parent company bears secondary liability with its subsidiary for transactions which the subsidiary entered into upon instructions from the parent company provided that the latter had a right to give such instructions.

2.20.11 Insolvency

[127] A Kazakhstan company that is insolvent is likely to be put into bankruptcy. While there is a rehabilitation procedure provided under Kazakhstan law, it is not often used. Therefore, the main implication when buying shares or interests of a company that is insolvent is that the acquirer should only do so if it is prepared either to make contributions to the capital of such company or otherwise finance such company to enable it to pay its debts.

[128] If the company is unable to pay its debts and goes into bankruptcy, it will be required to use its property to pay its creditors according to the order of priority established by law. Once it has done so it will be liquidated, with the shareholders or participants receiving any remaining property.

2.20.12 Choice of Law

[129] Kazakhstan law generally recognizes the choice of law, jurisdiction and arbitration clauses in contractual arrangements subject to the following.

[130] Under Kazakhstan law, agreements that involve at least one party that is not a Kazakhstan person, or that are otherwise 'complicated by a foreign element', are permitted to be governed by the laws of jurisdictions other than Kazakhstan. However, even if there is a foreign element, there are cases when Kazakhstan legislation prohibits the application of foreign law (e.g., when foreign law contravenes public order) or provides for the imperative application of Kazakhstan law (e.g., subject matter which must be governed by Kazakhstan law includes agreements related to immovable and other property registered in a state register in Kazakhstan). Thus, in practice, generally, contracts may be governed by foreign law where there is a foreign counterparty or the agreement has a 'foreign element'.

[131] Disputes between Kazakhstan persons are generally settled by Kazakhstan courts or by arbitration in Kazakhstan.

[132] The parties to an agreement may agree to submit disputes arising out of the agreement to the courts or the arbitration of a jurisdiction other than Kazakhstan, except for cases when Kazakhstan law provides otherwise (e.g., cases relating to rights to immovable property located in Kazakhstan).

2.20.13 Enforceability of Foreign Judgments

[133] Kazakhstan courts will enforce a judgment rendered by a court that is established in a foreign jurisdiction (i) in cases where such enforcement is expressly stipulated by law, or (ii) if there is an applicable treaty between Kazakhstan and such foreign jurisdiction that provides for the reciprocal enforcement of court judgments, or (iii) based on the principle of reciprocity. Under a reasonable interpretation, the principle of reciprocity means that a foreign judgment will be enforced in Kazakhstan if judgments of Kazakhstan courts are enforced in the relevant foreign country. It is assumed that judgments of Kazakhstan courts are enforced in a foreign country unless proven otherwise.

2.20.14 Enforceability of Foreign Arbitral Awards

[134] Under Kazakhstan law, Foreign Arbitral Awards can be enforced in Kazakhstan (i) in cases where such enforcement is expressly stipulated by law, or (ii) if there is an applicable treaty between Kazakhstan and such foreign jurisdiction that provides for reciprocal enforcement of arbitral awards, or (iii) based on the principle of reciprocity.

Kazakhstan is a party to the New York Convention.[16] The New York Convention is currently in force in Kazakhstan. Therefore, an arbitral award that is rendered in a New York Convention participating state (including the UK and the US) will generally be recognized and enforced in Kazakhstan provided that the conditions for enforcement set out in the New York Convention are met and the award is filed with the relevant Kazakhstan court for recognition and enforcement of the award in accordance with the Civil Procedural Code,[17] which provides statutory guidelines for the enforcement of arbitral awards under the conditions set out in the New York Convention.

[135] As regards arbitral awards rendered in foreign countries which are not New York Convention participating states – such awards are enforced in Kazakhstan (i) in cases where such enforcement is expressly stipulated by law, or (ii) if an applicable treaty between Kazakhstan and such foreign jurisdiction provides for the reciprocal enforcement of arbitral awards, or (iii) based on the principle of reciprocity. Under a reasonable interpretation, the principle of reciprocity means that an arbitral award rendered in a foreign country will be enforced in Kazakhstan provided arbitral awards rendered in Kazakhstan are enforced in the relevant foreign

---

[16] Convention on the Recognition and Enforcement of Foreign Arbitral Awards dated 10 Jun. 1958, New York (the *New York Convention*).

[17] Civil Procedural Code of the Republic of Kazakhstan No. 377-V dated 31 Oct. 2015, as amended (the *Civil Procedural Code*).

country. It is assumed that arbitral awards rendered in Kazakhstan are enforced in a foreign country unless proven otherwise.

2.21 Specific Rules on Public Takeovers

[136] There are no specific rules in Kazakhstan addressing public takeovers.

[137] Under the JSC Law, an investor who, acting either alone or jointly with its affiliated persons, is acquiring:

(1) about 30% or more of the voting shares of the JSC; or
(2) any other number of voting shares of the JSC, where such acquisition would result in such person alone or jointly with its affiliated persons holding 30% or more of the voting shares of the JSC;
(3) is required to make an offer to the remaining shareholders to buy out their shares at a price determined by the acquirer on the basis of the guidelines provided for in the JSC Law.

[138] Any failure by the acquirer to make such an offer would result in the acquirer being obliged to reduce its shareholding to not more than 29% of the company's voting shares.

[139] Any investor who, acting alone or jointly with its affiliated persons, acquires 95 or more per cent of the voting shares of a company, has a right to demand that the other remaining shareholders of the company (i.e., the minority shareholders) sell their voting shares in the company to him/them.

2.22 Other Relevant Laws and Due Diligence Issues

2.22.1 Anti-corruption Legislation

[140] Anti-corruption legislation is established in the Anti-Corruption Law.[18] Corruption is defined in the law as the illegal use of powers and opportunities related to them by (i) persons holding responsible public positions, (ii) persons authorized to perform public functions, (iii) persons equated to the persons authorized to perform public functions, or (iv) public officials, in order to receive personally or through intermediaries property (or non-property) benefits and advantages for themselves or for third parties, as well as the bribery of such persons. The law applies to all individuals and legal entities operating in Kazakhstan. Outside Kazakhstan, the law applies to Kazakhstan citizens and legal entities registered in Kazakhstan unless otherwise provided under international treaties.

---

[18] Law of the Republic of Kazakhstan 'On Combating Corruption' No. 410-V dated 18 Nov. 2015, as amended (the *Anti-Corruption Law*).

[141] Kazakhstan also ratified the UN Convention on Combating Corruption dated 31 October 2003.

[142] According to Transparency International's 2020 ranking on corruption, Kazakhstan is ranked 94th out of 180 countries in the world (113th in 2019).

[143] The Anti-Money Laundering Law[19] sets out measures directed toward countering money laundering and financing, including financial monitoring of suspicious monetary transactions.

[144] Suspicious monetary transactions are subject to financial monitoring regardless of the amount of money involved. A suspicious monetary transaction is a transaction where money or property used to execute the transaction is suspected to be a profit from criminal activity or the transaction is directed toward legalization (laundering) of profits from criminal activity or toward financing terrorism.

[145] The Anti-Money Laundering Law requires certain entities to carry out screening and other actions aimed at preventing money laundering activities. Such entities include, *inter alia*, banks, stock exchanges, insurance brokers and insurance companies, pension funds, notaries, legal advisors, audit organizations, gambling and lottery organizations, microfinance organizations and operators of transfers of funds.

[146] Under the Anti-Money Laundering Law, these entities must monitor, *inter alia*, transactions for the exchange of currencies, transfers of funds, operations involving bank accounts, insurance payments, transactions involving refined precious metals, immovable property transactions, service agreements and transactions with securities. These entities must also monitor their new clients and counterparties.

[147] Where the US or other international investors that are subject to the Foreign Corrupt Practices Act (FCPA) or UK Bribery Act are involved in transactions in Kazakhstan, may ask for particular representations or provisions indicating that their Kazakhstan counterparts have not engaged in any actions that would violate such laws. Generally, however, such laws have not had a noticeable impact on M&A transactions in Kazakhstan.

2.22.2 Environmental Legislation and IP Rights

[148] In 2021, Kazakhstan adopted a new Environmental Code,[20] which became effective starting July 2021 and applies to legal relations arising after its entry into force. The Environmental Code regulates environmental protection issues in Kazakhstan. In most cases, when undertaking due diligence, it is necessary to check the compliance of a company's activities with environmental legislation.

---

[19] Law of the Republic of Kazakhstan 'On Combating Money Laundering Obtained by Illegal Means and Terrorism Financing No. 191-IV' dated 28 Aug. 2009, as amended (the *Anti-Money Laundering Law*).

[20] Environmental Code of the Republic of Kazakhstan No. 400-VI dated 2 Jan. 2021, as amended (the *Environmental Code*).

[149] Intellectual property rights, including patents, trademarks, copyrights, reproduction rights, broadcasting rights and trade secrets are protected by the Copyright Law,[21] the Trademark Law[22] and the Patent Law.[23] Although there is no specific Kazakhstan law on trade secrets, they are generally protected under Article 126 of the Civil Code. The principal state agency involved in the registration of matters pertaining to copyrights, inventions, utility models, industrial designs, trademarks and service marks is the Ministry of Justice. Kazakhstan is a party to a number of international treaties including, *inter alia*, the Paris Convention for the Protection of Industrial Property, the Madrid Agreement Concerning the International Registration of Trade Marks and the Patent Cooperation Treaty.

2.22.3 Agents Rights

[150] In cases of early termination, agents performing services under agency agreements are entitled to recover expenses incurred by the agent prior to termination and its fees (if any) proportionate to the amount of work already performed. Indemnities in Kazakhstan are limited to compensation of damages only.

2.22.4 Change of Control Provisions

[151] Change of control provisions are frequently used in many types of agreements in Kazakhstan. This includes finance/loan documents as well as many types of contracts. Such provisions are enforceable and, when undertaking due diligence in connection with an acquisition, this is a key issue to look for so that it can be addressed by the parties before completing the acquisition.

2.23 The Due Diligence Process

[152] Due diligence investigations involving commercial, financial, tax, property, environmental and other issues are common and sellers are usually familiar with such processes. While property issues are usually investigated as part of due diligence, usually reliance is placed on reviewing documents provided by the seller rather than an independent search of the records.

[153] Both virtual and physical data rooms are used, though for large transactions virtual data rooms are becoming the norm.

[154] Critical issues when conducting due diligence in Kazakhstan very much depend on the sector in which the target company operates. For transactions in the

---

[21] Law of the Republic of Kazakhstan 'On Copyright and Associated Rights' No. 6-I dated 10 Jun. 1996, as amended (the *Copyright Law*).

[22] Law of the Republic of Kazakhstan 'On Trade Marks, Service Marks and Protected Designation of Origin' of the Republic of Kazakhstan No. 456-I dated 26 Jul. 1999, as amended (the *Trademark Law*).

[23] Law of the Republic of Kazakhstan 'On Patents' No. 427-I dated 16 Jul. 1999, as amended (the *Patent Law*).

mining and petroleum sectors, particular emphasis will be placed on investigating whether the subsurface user has met the obligations under its work programme for carrying out exploration and/or production. In addition, it is critical to investigate prior transfers of ownership of the assets to confirm that all necessary consents were given. In each case, the failure to have fulfilled obligations or to have obtained consents can lead to the termination of the subsurface use rights (i.e., the exploration or production contract) involved.

[155] The imposition of contractual representations, warranties and indemnities is common. While such concepts are not explicitly provided for by Kazakhstan law, these are often used in transaction documents (especially, in high-value deals) drafted under both Kazakhstan and foreign law to address particular issues found during due diligence. Because Kazakhstan law does not explicitly recognize representations, warranties and indemnities, the enforceability of such provisions where the agreements are governed by Kazakhstan law is less certain than if a foreign law is used to govern the transaction.

2.24 Role of the Courts

[156] Disputes between Kazakhstan persons and/or legal entities are generally settled by Kazakhstan courts or Kazakhstan arbitration courts. Kazakhstan law also provides for various pre-court and out-of-court procedures (settlement agreements, participative procedure agreements, mediation agreements, etc.).

[157] The parties to an agreement may agree to submit disputes arising out of the agreement to the courts or arbitration courts of a jurisdiction other than Kazakhstan, except for cases when Kazakhstan law provides otherwise (e.g., cases relating to rights to immovable property located in Kazakhstan). Since 2017, in cases where it is not prohibited by law, a dispute (conflict) arising from civil law relations by written agreement of the parties may be resolved through the court of the AIFC. The AIFC Court represents a judicial system based on the rules and principles of English common law. It has exclusive jurisdiction over disputes arising from the activities of the AIFC, as well as in respect of disputes referred to the AIFC Court by agreement of the parties. The AIFC Court is independent in its activities and is not part of the judicial system of the Republic of Kazakhstan. The AIFC Court has its own procedural rules, which were drawn up on the basis of the norms and principles of English common law. In addition, there is a special fast track procedure for small claims.

[158] The Kazakhstan judicial system is not fully independent and also may be subject to outside influence. Courts, and especially regional courts, are sometimes reluctant to issue judgments against local state authorities.

[159] Judgments by Kazakhstan courts and awards by local arbitration courts are enforceable. Decisions by local arbitration courts may be appealed to the local

courts based on specific grounds stipulated in the Arbitrage Law[24] (which are mostly related to procedural violations).

[160] Under Kazakhstan law, foreign court judgments and Foreign Arbitral Awards can be enforced in Kazakhstan (i) in cases where such enforcement is expressly stipulated by law, (ii) if there is an applicable treaty between Kazakhstan and such foreign jurisdiction that provides for reciprocal enforcement of court judgments and arbitral awards, or (iii) based on the principle of reciprocity.

[161] Kazakhstan is not a party to multilateral or bilateral treaties for the mutual enforcement of court judgments with most countries, except for a limited number of treaties primarily with CIS countries.

[162] Kazakhstan is a signatory to the New York Convention. Therefore, an arbitral award that is rendered in a New York Convention participating state (including the UK and the USA) will generally be recognized and enforced in Kazakhstan provided that the conditions for enforcement set out in the New York Convention are met and the award is filed with the relevant Kazakhstan court for recognition and enforcement of the award in accordance with the Civil Procedural Code, which provides statutory guidelines for the enforcement of arbitral awards.

[163] The principle of reciprocity, under reasonable interpretation, means that a court judgment and an arbitral award rendered in a foreign country are enforced in Kazakhstan provided a court judgment and an arbitral award rendered in Kazakhstan are enforced in the relevant foreign country. It is assumed that court judgments and arbitral awards rendered in Kazakhstan are enforced in a foreign country unless proven otherwise.

[164] Foreign companies have successfully obtained judgments and awards against state authorities and local companies before domestic courts. For example, foreign companies have been successful in disputes involving taxes, payment of duties, claims against imposed fines and contractual disputes.

[165] Although it is possible to include into a contract a restrictive covenant not to compete with a business sold, it is doubtful whether such provisions will be enforced in Kazakhstan. Moreover, we believe that there is a risk that a court or the state authorities would consider such a restrictive covenant as an anticompetitive agreement and a violation of competition laws.

[166] Confidential information and trade secrets may well be safeguarded by confidentiality provisions. Such provisions are enforceable in Kazakhstan, generally.

[167] In reality, there are very few protections available to minority investors.

[168] Kazakhstan law has no concept of warranties and indemnities. Therefore, it is unlikely that warranties and indemnities as known in the UK or similar jurisdictions will be enforced in Kazakhstan if provided for in a Kazakhstan law-governed agreement. However, such provisions can be drafted in a way that will increase the

---

[24] Law of the Republic of Kazakhstan 'On Arbitrage' No. 488-V dated 8 Apr. 2016, as amended (the *Arbitrage Law*).

chances of them being enforced and which can give rise to an enforceable claim by one party against another.

[169] Courts in Kazakhstan are relatively efficient and claims in courts can be pursued relatively fast, based on statutory time limits for consideration of claims in courts. It is not generally an expensive process although most claims require payment of state duty in the amount of 3% of the value of the claim.

3 MERGER CONTROLS: ANTITRUST/ COMPETITION ISSUES

3.1 Relevant Legislation and Competent Authorities

[170] The merger control regime in Kazakhstan is established pursuant to the Entrepreneurial Code. The relevant authority is the Antimonopoly Agency.

[171] For most transactions, the merger control regime requires prior consent from the Antimonopoly Agency for 'economic concentration'. Some transactions require notification of the Antimonopoly Agency subsequent to the execution of the transaction. The consent and notification requirements are mandatory but they do not apply to transactions which do not meet the requirements established by the Entrepreneurial Code.

[172] The consent of the Antimonopoly Agency is valid for a period of one year from the date the consent was given. If the transaction has not been completed within one year, the applicant must submit a new application to the Antimonopoly Agency.

3.2 Prior Consent

[173] Subject to the tests specified below, prior consent of the Antimonopoly Agency is required in respect of:

(1) reorganization of a company through a merger or accession to another company;
(2) acquisition of voting shares/participating interests in a company that brings the amount of its ownership in such company to over 50% of its voting shares/participating interests provided that prior to the acquisition the acquirer owned 50% or less of the voting shares/participating interests in that company; and
(3) acquisition, taking possession or use of the fixed and/or intangible assets of another company, provided that the book value of such assets exceeds 10% of the book value of the fixed and intangible assets of the company disposing of or transferring such assets.

3.3 Notification

[174] In some limited cases, prior consent is not needed but instead, subsequent notification of the Antimonopoly Agency is required. Subject to the tests specified below, subsequent notification of the Antimonopoly Agency is required to be made for:

(1) the acquisition of rights (including where based on trust management, joint activities or a commission agreement) which enable the acquirer to give mandatory instructions to another entity relating to its business activity or to carry out functions of its executive body; and

(2) participation of the same individuals in the executive bodies, boards of directors, supervisory councils or other governing bodies of two or more market entities provided that such individuals determine the conditions for conducting business activity by such market entities.

3.4 General Merger Control Tests

[175] The consent or notification of the Antimonopoly Agency for the above transactions is required if the aggregate balance sheet value of the assets or the aggregate volume of sales of goods (works, services) of the acquirer and its group of entities (including the target company whose shares/participating interests will be acquired) for the last financial year, exceeds 10 million times the MCI (currently KZT29 470 000 000 or approximately USD68 534 884) that is in effect on the date of submission of the application for consent/notification.

3.5 Merger Control Test for Financial Institutions

[176] Where one of the parties is a financial institution (e.g., a bank, a broker, a dealer, etc.), the consent or notification of the Antimonopoly Agency is required if:

(1) the value of assets or equity capital of the financial institution exceeds the limits set by the Antimonopoly Agency in cooperation with the Agency for Regulation and Development of the Financial Market of Kazakhstan;

(2) the financial institution holds a dominant or monopolistic position and meets the General Merger Control Test.

3.6 Exemptions from the Merger Control Rule

[177] Certain transactions are not considered to be economic concentrations and therefore consent/notification of the Antimonopoly Agency is not required for their execution. These include:

(1) acquisition of shares/participating interests by financial institutions undertaken for subsequent resale provided that such financial institutions are not entitled to vote in the management bodies of the target company;

(2) acquisition by financial organizations of any property/assets of another company for their subsequent resale with a view to discharging the debtor's obligations in full or in part;

(3) appointment of a rehabilitation or a bankruptcy manager or an interim (provisional) administrator;

(4) transactions carried out within one group of persons.

3.7 Procedure and Timing of Notification and Obtaining Consent

[178] To receive consent from the Antimonopoly Agency, the acquirer must submit a formal application containing full and correct information and supporting documents required under the Entrepreneurial Code.

[179] The Antimonopoly Agency has ten calendar days from the date of submission of the application to decide whether all necessary information and documents are provided and can be accepted for review. If any required information and/or documents are missing or do not meet the formalities, the Antimonopoly Agency will return the application to the acquirer. In such a case, the acquirer has the right to submit a new application which should be free of the defects specified by the Antimonopoly Agency.

[180] If the Antimonopoly Agency accepts the application, it will then have thirty calendar days to decide whether to give its consent. The Antimonopoly Agency, however, has the right to suspend the review process if it needs additional information and/or documents from the acquirer or other state authorities. In such cases, the Antimonopoly Agency notifies the applicant about the suspension of consideration of the application. For example, acquisition of subsurface use rights or shares/participating interests in companies engaging directly or indirectly in subsurface use (i.e., mining and oil & gas companies) requires a waiver of the state's priority right and the consent of the competent state authority. Consideration of an application can also be suspended in case it is necessary to conduct an analysis of competition conditions on commodity markets. The Antimonopoly Agency may suspend consideration of the application until the waiver and consent have been received and provided to it, or until the analysis is completed.

[181] Under the Entrepreneurial Code, consent must be issued by the Antimonopoly Agency within approximately forty calendar days of submission of the application. However, given the time needed to prepare the application and supporting documents and the right of the Antimonopoly Agency to suspend consideration of the application, the process in practice takes three months or more.

[182] Given the above, it is usually helpful to start gathering all documents and information as soon as possible. As the acceptance of the application can be refused on formal grounds, it is often advisable to hire experienced external advisors to help prepare the application. The common practice in Kazakhstan is to make the consent of the Antimonopoly Agency a condition precedent to the closing of the transaction. It is possible to obtain the consent of the Antimonopoly Agency on the basis of a draft sale and purchase agreement.

[183] If a transaction involves the acquisition of shares on a stock exchange, then the application can be submitted either before the transaction on the exchange or within thirty calendar days after the purchase of shares on the exchange.

[184] If a transaction is subject to notification, the notification to the Antimonopoly Agency must be sent not later than forty-five calendar days following the date of execution of the transaction. If the Antimonopoly Agency does not issue an order to cancel the transaction within thirty calendar days from the date the Antimonopoly Agency received the notification, then the economic concentration is deemed to have been completed.

3.8 Deals That Can Be Refused/Rejected

[185] The Antimonopoly Agency may refuse consent if it finds that execution of a relevant transaction will result in restriction of competition in Kazakhstan. Because it is difficult to prove that a relevant transaction will result in the restriction of competition in Kazakhstan, in most cases the Antimonopoly Agency gives its consent to transactions. If the Antimonopoly Agency refuses to issue the consent, it must specify the reasons for such refusal. In certain cases, the Antimonopoly Agency may grant its consent subject to certain conditions and obligations on the participants in the transaction. Such conditions and obligations should be aimed at eliminating or mitigating the negative influence caused by the economic concentration on competition in Kazakhstan. They may include limitations on management or use of assets, or conduct of business, or may require disposal of certain assets.

[186] If following the review of a notification on economic concentration, the Antimonopoly Agency considers that the transaction resulted or can result in limitation or elimination of competition, the Antimonopoly Agency issues an order requiring the elimination of violations of the Entrepreneurial Code. Such order must be fulfilled within thirty calendar days and can be enforced through the courts. The Entrepreneurial Code does not specify which actions can be required under the order. Presumably, the Antimonopoly Agency can require a limitation on the use of assets, or the conduct of a business, or even the termination of a transaction.

[187] If the acquirer believes that the Antimonopoly Agency may issue an order as mentioned above, then the acquirer can seek prior consent before the execution of the transaction instead of notification.

[188] Under the Entrepreneurial Code, competitors and other stakeholders in the target company do not have any role when the Antimonopoly Agency makes a decision on an application.

3.9 Sanctions for Breaching the Merger Control Rules

[189] If an antimonopoly consent is required but not obtained, then the transaction itself is not invalid per se as a matter of Kazakhstan law. A court decision is required in order to invalidate the transaction. The legal basis for invalidation of a transaction exists if a person (entity) fails to obtain the consent of the Antimonopoly Agency for an economic concentration that results in the emergence or strengthening of a dominant or a monopoly position of a market entity and/or a limitation of competition. State registration or re-registration of a legal entity, or rights to real estate which were carried out without obtaining consent, can also be invalidated through the courts.

[190] In circumstances where antimonopoly consent is not received for a transaction involving a foreign acquirer and a foreign target company that directly or indirectly controls a Kazakhstan company, Kazakhstan legislation does not establish any specific mechanism or procedures for enforcing the decisions of the Antimonopoly Agency or of the Kazakhstan courts. We are not aware of any cases of invalidation of such transactions for not receiving antimonopoly consent.

[191] Failure to obtain the consent of or to notify the Antimonopoly Agency about the relevant transaction may result in the imposition of an administrative fine on the acquirer in a range from 80 MCI to 1 600 MCI (currently from KZT233 3600 to KZT4 667 200 or approximately from USD543 to USD10 854).

3.10 Anticompetitive Restraints

[192] It is normal to prevent the vendor and/or key employees from competing with the business sold or from soliciting key employees of the business being sold. However, Kazakhstan law generally does not support such restrictions.

[193] A non-compete clause may be viewed by the Antimonopoly Agency as a violation of the prohibition on anticompetitive agreements as it limits the access of other entities to the market.

[194] Under Kazakhstan law, an employer may conclude an agreement on non-competition with its employees under which the employees are obliged not to carry out actions that 'may damage the employer'. Since the concept of non-competition in the context of employment is relatively new for Kazakhstan law, the court practice on enforcement of non-competition agreements varies.

4 TAXATION ASPECTS

4.1 Nature of the Tax Regime

[195] In general, the Kazakhstan tax regime may be regarded as a certain tax environment. The tax system is, generally, transparent and the rules are most often simple. However, certain rules are ambiguous and often not properly applied. In addition, the tax authorities aggressively enforce tax legislation. As a result, occasionally taxpayers are dependent on the interpretation of the rules by the tax authorities and such interpretation may be inconsistent. In addition, the tax regime is in a relatively early stage of its development compared to countries with established market economies and the tax authorities often do not fully understand the legislation. Therefore, the tax risks involved in doing business in Kazakhstan may be more significant than those in jurisdictions with a more developed legal and tax system.

[196] The Kazakhstan tax regime is established under the Tax Code[25] and normative legal acts the adoption of which are explicitly provided under the Tax Code. The Tax Code is aimed at enhancement of the existing tax policy, improvement of tax administration and efficiency of tax-related services provided by the state.

4.2 Liability to Tax

[197] Under the Tax Code, companies working in Kazakhstan (including branches and representatives of foreign legal entities) may be subject to the following taxes:

- CIT;
- withholding tax on payments to non-residents;
- VAT;
- excise tax (if applicable);
- social taxes for employees;
- property tax;
- land tax;
- vehicle tax;
- export and import duties; and
- other obligatory payments to the budget.

[198] In addition, a special set of taxes applies to subsurface users (as discussed below).

---

[25] Code of the Republic of Kazakhstan 'On taxes and other obligatory payments to the budget (Tax Code)' dated 25 December 2017 No. 120-VI, as amended ('Tax Code').

4.3 Tax Implications for Foreign Legal Entities in Kazakhstan

[199] There are two basic ways in which a foreign legal entity may be subject to Kazakhstan taxation. First, if they become a *PE*, which can include a branch, representative office, construction site, installation, assembly site, provision of services or performance of supervisory activities associated with the production of natural resources, etc. Second, even if a foreign legal entity does not have a PE, it may still be subject to taxation if it receives Kazakhstan source income as defined in the legislation.

[200] For the purposes of taxation in Kazakhstan, representative offices and branches are regarded as non-residents with a registered presence in Kazakhstan. Both are subject to taxation in Kazakhstan.

[201] Kazakhstan tax law allows non-resident legal entities which engage in activities that create a PE in Kazakhstan to register as a taxpayer with the tax authorities in Kazakhstan without registering a branch or a representative office in Kazakhstan. Although non-resident legal entities which engage in activities that create a PE in Kazakhstan are required to register with the tax authorities in Kazakhstan, the existence of a PE is not dependent on registration with the authorities. If a non-resident engages in activities that create a PE in Kazakhstan, it is deemed to be subject to taxation whether or not it registers as a taxpayer with the tax authorities or registers a PE with the Non-Commercial Joint-Stock Company "State Corporation "Government for Citizens".

[202] The taxes mentioned above have their own separate filing and reporting requirements. A legal entity or a registered PE in Kazakhstan is required to maintain its accounting books in accordance with the International Financial Reporting Standards (IFRS) or National Accounting Standards (as applicable) depending on the size of the business[26] and in the state and (or) Russian language.

4.4 Corporate Income Tax

[203] For tax purposes, Kazakhstan legal entities, including subsidiaries of foreign legal entities, are regarded as tax residents, and branches and representative offices of foreign entities are regarded as non-residents. Non-residents are taxable only on their Kazakhstan source income, while residents are subject to CIT on their worldwide income (subject, of course, to the application of double tax treaties (DTTs), where applicable). This means that in addition to Kazakhstan source income, residents are required to include income received from sources outside of Kazakhstan.

---

[26] Large- and medium-sized enterprises shall maintain their accounting books in accordance with IFRS, while small enterprises in accordance with National Accounting Standards.

[204] The CIT rate in Kazakhstan is a flat 20% in 2021. The tax base for CIT is net taxable profit, which is computed as the difference between taxable revenues and deductible expenses.

[205] For CIT purposes, a taxpayer can claim a tax deduction for costs incurred to generate business revenues, including (i) payroll costs, (ii) depreciation and amortization of fixed and intangible assets, (iii) capital expenditures in respect of certain types of buildings (including certain industrial construction, equipment, etc.) and fixed assets, (iv) lease payments, (v) various service fees, (vi) interest expense, and (vii) other costs of doing business. Most expenses can be deducted without any limits, but some costs such as interest and business trip expenses have deductibility limits. All expenses for which a tax deduction in Kazakhstan are claimed must be supported by source documents such as invoices, receipts, contracts, etc.

[206] Net taxable profit can be reduced by the amount of net operating losses carried forward from past periods. Net operating losses can be carried forward for ten consecutive years.

4.5 Branch Office

[207] A branch is subject to all applicable taxes in Kazakhstan. It is subject to CIT only for the income it earns from sources within Kazakhstan. Under most of Kazakhstan's DTTs, a branch can claim a tax deduction for a portion of the overhead expenses that its head office incurs.

[208] In addition to CIT, branches of foreign legal entities are subject to a branch profits tax. This tax applies to after-tax profits of branches at a rate of 15% but is reduced by most of Kazakhstan's tax treaties with other countries to 5%.

4.6 Value Added Tax

[209] The standard VAT rate is 12% for 2021. It applies to revenues derived from the sale of goods or services within Kazakhstan and to imports of goods and services into Kazakhstan. Nil rate VAT applies to exports of goods from the Eurasian Economic Union and international transportation services.

4.7 Subsurface Use-Related Taxes

[210] Under the Tax Code, the current tax regime for subsurface users is as follows.

4.8 Signature Bonus

[211] Signature bonus is a one-time fixed payment of a subsurface user who has concluded a subsurface use contract (except for a subsurface use contract for production concluded as a result of commercial discovery within the exploration stage). The amount of a signature bonus depends on a range of factors, including the type of subsurface use contract, the type of mineral resources and the availability of approved reserves.

4.9 Compensation of Historical Costs

[212] A subsurface user has to make a fixed payment to reimburse the state for historical costs incurred by the state for geological surveys and for the development of the contract territory prior to the conclusion of the subsurface use contract.

4.10 Mineral Extraction Tax

[213] Subsurface users who extract crude oil, gas (condensate and natural gas), minerals, underground waters and therapeutic mud (*minerals*) are subject to payment of the Mineral Extraction Tax (MET). The MET is paid by the subsurface user separately for each type of mineral. The physical volume of the produced minerals is recognized as the tax base.

[214] The MET for crude oil is payable at rates ranging from 5% to 18% depending on the annual physical volume of production. For domestic sales of crude oil and gas condensate, the above MET rates are decreased by 50%.

[215] The MET for raw gas is 10%. For domestic sales of natural gas, the MET rates range from 0.5% to 1.5% depending on the annual physical volume of production.

[216] The MET for different types of mineral resources contained in the mineral raw materials, such as coal, gold, silver, copper, etc., ranges from 0% to 18.5%.

4.11 Excess Profit Tax

[217] Excess Profit Tax (EPT) applies to all subsurface users, except in relation to the following subsurface use contracts:

(1) production sharing agreements concluded prior to 1 January 2009 which provide for a tax stabilization regime, and which passed the obligatory tax expertise, and were approved by the Kazakhstan President;

(2) subsurface use contracts for exploration and (or) production of widespread solid minerals, underground waters and (or) therapeutic mud provided they do not envision the production of other mineral resources;

(3) contracts for construction and operation of underground facilities not connected with exploration and production.

[218] EPT is paid on a sliding scale tax rate from 0% to 60% depending on the amount of net income within certain thresholds.

4.12 Personal Income Tax

[219] Kazakhstan employers (i.e., Kazakhstan legal entities, subsidiaries of foreign entities, branch and representative offices of foreign legal entities) are regarded as tax agents and are required to withhold personal income tax (PIT) and remit it to the state from payments they make to their employees in cash or in kind. In general, all types of compensation and benefits that an employee receives for employment services constitute taxable employment income. The PIT rate applicable to resident and non-resident employees in Kazakhstan is flat and amounts to 10% of taxable employment income.

4.13 Social Tax

[220] Kazakhstan employers are required to pay social tax for their employees. The social tax is borne entirely by the employer and no portion of it is withheld from employee salaries.

[221] From 1 January 2018, the social tax applies at a flat rate of 9.5% and from 1 January 2025 will apply at a flat rate of 11% to the gross income of employees, including all fringe benefits, whether received in cash or in kind. There is no maximum threshold for the social tax base. Obligatory contributions to pension funds in Kazakhstan and a few other minor allowances such as compensation for unused vacation are exempt from social tax.

4.14 Social Security Contributions

[222] Kazakhstan employers must make contributions to the State Social Security Fund for their local employees, including foreign citizens who are permanent residents of Kazakhstan. A foreign employee without a permanent residence permit is not subject to this contribution requirement.

[223] Social security contributions apply to employees' monthly gross salaries and are calculated at a rate of 3.5% of an individual's gross salary. There is a limit established for an individual's monthly social security contribution, which is KZT10 413 or approximately USD24. Social security contributions are fully creditable against

social tax and, therefore, do not represent an additional tax burden for an employer.

4.15 Obligatory Pension Contributions

[224] Kazakhstan nationals and foreign citizens with residence permits (but not those foreign citizens on a work visa) must pay 10% of their gross salaries as obligatory pension contributions to the state-owned pension fund, Unified Accumulative Pension Fund JSC (UAPF). Kazakhstan registered taxpayers that make payments to local nationals must withhold pension contributions from the amounts due to the employees and remit these amounts to the pension fund. The current upper limit on monthly mandatory pension contributions is KZT212 500 or approximately USD494 at the current exchange rate. Contributions to the UAPF are deductible for PIT purposes. In addition, from 1 January 2014, employers are obliged to make additional contributions in the amount of 5% of employees' salaries to the UAPF for those employees who perform their employment duties in hazardous conditions (e.g., employees working in mines). The list of positions entitled to such additional contributions is approved by the Kazakhstan Government on an annual basis.

4.16 Property, Vehicle and Land Taxes

[225] Companies that own buildings and certain structures which are recorded in books as fixed assets, or investments in a property under international accounting standards, and Kazakhstan legislation on accounting and financial statements are subject to property tax.

[226] The property tax rate for property owned by legal entities is 1.5% (except for a few categories of non-commercial legal entities) and applies to the average annual book value of the taxable assets. Property tax applies regardless of whether profit is derived from the use of the assets.

[227] Vehicles registered in Kazakhstan are subject to an annual vehicle tax. The vehicle tax rate depends on the vehicle's engine volume and age.

[228] Land tax applies if an entity owns or uses land in Kazakhstan. The land tax rate depends on the land quality and category and is established in the form of annual fixed payments per unit of land area.

4.17 Customs Duties

[229] On 27 November 2009, Russia, Belarus and Kazakhstan announced the establishment of a single customs territory of the customs union of the said three states which came into force on 1 July 2010. The Customs Union aims to create a

single market and to encourage trade and investment by eliminating administrative barriers and the simplification of customs procedures within the Customs Union. The territory of the Customs Union is now treated as a single customs territory, within which customs duties and economic restrictions do not apply as between the participants of the Customs Union. Exceptions to this agreement include special protective, antidumping and countervailing measures. The Customs Union also enforces a single customs tariff and other common measures to regulate the trade of goods with third party countries.

[230] The parties to the Customs Union took further steps to strengthen their mutual cooperation by entering into an agreement on the Eurasian Economic Union on 29 May 2014, which eliminates any customs duties for the transportation of goods between the Member States (Russia, Belarus, Kazakhstan, Armenia and Kyrgyzstan).

[231] The customs duties applicable to transactions with non-members of the Eurasian Economic Union include the following payments:

(1) import and export duties, the amount of which depends on the type of goods;
(2) VAT of 12% for the import of goods;
(3) excise tax for the import of goods, the amount of which depends on the type of goods; and
(4) other fees for customs declaration of goods, customs escort and the preliminary decision of customs authorities.

[232] The export and import of certain types of goods may require a licence under Kazakhstan licensing legislation. Licences for import or export are generally issued for a period of up to one calendar year for different types of goods and for separate transactions. Goods that require a licence for import or export include, *inter alia*, hazardous waste, nuclear materials, some medical equipment, cryptographic facilities, subsurface information and rare metals.

4.18 Other Payments

[233] Various other fees and levies may apply to certain types of activity in Kazakhstan. For example, there are fees for registration of real estate transactions, environmental pollution charges and stamp duties for actions performed by governmental bodies such as notarization and court fees. In addition, companies may need to pay a licence fee for the right to engage in certain specified types of activities such as construction, exploration, drilling and production works.

4.19 Tax Consolidation Group Relief of Gains and Losses

[234] Under the Tax Code, all Kazakhstan companies must keep their tax accounting separately. As such, Kazakhstan companies would not have imputed their profits from a foreign subsidiary or impute their losses or gains elsewhere within the group.

4.20 Tax Considerations Arising from M&A Transactions

[235] The basic tax issues which arise for the principal parties on M&A transactions in Kazakhstan are capital gains tax, withholding tax on sales of shares/participating interests and VAT (in case of the acquisition of assets).

4.21 Capital Gain Tax Exemption

[236] Generally, all acquisitions and disposals of shares/participating interests in Kazakhstan companies are subject to a capital gain tax in Kazakhstan. Also, the net gain realized from the disposal of participating interests owned by or shares issued by a non-resident of Kazakhstan, where 50% or more of the value of such participating interests or shares is made up of assets situated in Kazakhstan, is subject to Kazakhstan withholding tax (WHT).

[237] However, the Tax Code provides that taxable income of residents might be decreased and non-residents might be relieved from capital gains tax in respect of the sales of shares/participating interests in one of the three cases below:

(1) if the seller (whether an individual or legal entity):
  – is not a resident of a country with a favourable tax regime (i.e., a tax haven). The exact list of countries with a favourable tax regime is approved by the Kazakhstan Government;
  – has held the shares or participating interests for more than three years as at the date of disposal;
  – the target company whose shares or participating interests are being sold is not a Kazakhstan subsurface user and more than 50% of the value of the assets of the target company is made up of property of entities which are not Kazakhstan subsurface users.
(2) if income is derived from 'open trade' sales of shares on the Kazakhstan Stock Exchange or a foreign stock exchange provided that such shares are admitted to the official list of such stock exchange at the time of sale;
(3) if income is derived from sales of shares issued by or participating interests in a legal entity, which is a participant of the international technology park "Astana Hub".

4.22 Capital Gain Tax on Disposal of Shares/ Participating Interests

[238] Unless the disposal qualifies for the Kazakhstan tax exemption as described above, a disposal of shares/participating interests will be taxed as follows.

4.23 Treatment of Seller

[239] Generally, the sale of shares/participating interests in a Kazakhstan company by a non-resident to another non-resident or to a Kazakhstan resident is subject to withholding tax in Kazakhstan at the rate of 15%. If the seller is registered in a country with a favourable tax regime, the net gain realized from the disposal of the shares or participating interests is subject to withholding tax at the rate of 20%. Withholding tax on the gains realized by a non-resident seller may be reduced or eliminated under an applicable double taxation treaty. Sale of shares/participating interests in a company, which is a participant of the international technology park "Astana Hub", is subject to withholding tax at the rate of 5%.

4.24 Treatment of Acquirer

[240] Any acquirer of shares or participating interests from a non-resident seller will be considered as a tax agent for withholding tax purposes. If the acquirer acting as a tax agent is a non-resident not subject to Kazakhstan taxation, then in order to fulfil its obligation to withhold and remit tax, the non-resident acquirer should register with the Kazakhstan tax authorities. The exception is in cases when the target company whose shares/participating interests are being sold is a Kazakhstan subsurface user. If the target company is a Kazakhstan subsurface user, the tax obligations on assessment, declaration, withholding and remittance of tax on capital gains can be fulfilled by the target company itself. A resident acquirer will be regarded as a tax agent and thus will be obliged to withhold capital gain tax if it purchases shares or participating interests in a Kazakhstan company from a non-resident.

4.25 VAT on Shares/Participating Interests Sale

[241] The sale of shares or participating interests is exempt from Kazakhstan VAT of 12%.

4.26 Sale of Assets

[242] A sale of Kazakhstan assets which are subject to registration with the state authorities in Kazakhstan by a non-resident to another non-resident or to a Kazakhstan resident may be subject to capital gain tax in Kazakhstan at the tax rates discussed above (i.e., withholding tax at the rate of 15%, or 20% if the seller is registered in a country with a favourable tax regime).

[243] Generally, the sale of Kazakhstan assets (e.g., subsurface use rights under a subsurface use contract, immovable and movable property or the enterprise as it is) triggers Kazakhstan VAT of 12%, regardless of whether the seller is a resident or non-resident. The VAT tax base is normally determined as a contractually agreed sale price.

4.27 Structuring the Investment: Withholding Taxes

[244] Generally, all payments made by a Kazakhstan resident to a non-resident that constitute income are subject to withholding tax under the Tax Code.

4.28 Withholding Tax Application with No Double Tax Treaty

[245] WHT applies to the so-called Kazakhstan source income and is collected by the Kazakhstan entity making payment to a non-resident legal entity which does not have a PE in Kazakhstan. Kazakhstan legislation provides for a rather broad definition of Kazakhstan source income. Generally, it includes all services physically performed within Kazakhstan as well as certain types of services rendered outside of Kazakhstan (e.g., management consulting services provided by non-residents to residents of Kazakhstan).

[246] The income paid to a non-resident entity for services rendered in Kazakhstan is subject to WHT at the time of payment. The standard WHT rate for services (including for management or consultancy fees paid to foreign shareholders or affiliates and payments relating to the renting of immovable property in Kazakhstan) is 20% of the gross amount invoiced. However, certain services might be subject to different rates, as discussed below. There are also certain tax exemptions that can be applied to certain types of income.

[247] WHT at the rate of 15% is applied on income from (i) capital gains (on the sale of shares/participating interests and assets located in Kazakhstan, which are required to obtain a state registration), (ii) dividends payable to foreign shareholders (both individuals and companies), (iii) royalties (i.e., fees related to the usage of IP rights, trademarks, software, licences and patent fees, know-how rights, etc.), (iv) interest on loans (credits), or (v) insurance premiums under insurance policies.

[248] WHT at the rate of 5% is applied on income from (i) insurance premiums under reinsurance agreements, and (ii) international carriage services.

[249] However, if the payments (including those mentioned above) are made to a non-resident of a country with a favourable tax regime such payments will be subject to withholding tax at the rate of 20%.

4.29 Withholding Tax Application under a Double Tax Treaty

[250] The application of a DTT is available if the service supplier is a resident of a country which is a party to DTT with Kazakhstan. Kazakhstan has DTTs in more than forty countries. In accordance with most of these DTTs, income from certain types of activities should not be subject to taxation in Kazakhstan even if domestic legislation would seek to tax the income.

[251] Most DTTs also provide for a reduced rate of tax on certain income sources such as dividends, royalty and interest. At the time of payment of income to a non-resident, the tax agent may automatically apply the provisions of the relevant DTT based on a document presented by the non-resident to confirm his residency (the *Certificate of Residence*) where such resident is a beneficial recipient of the revenues and has the right to apply the provisions of such international agreement. The Certificate of Residence has to be in compliance with the requirements of the Tax Code with regard to apostille (the signature and stamp of the relevant authority and notary must be legalized). Additionally, copies of foundation documents of a non-resident legal entity must be provided by non-residents to the tax agent, so that the latter may apply the provisions of the relevant DTT at the time of payment.

[252] In practice, LLPs and JSCs are the most widely used types of entities in Kazakhstan. There are, however, no typical investment structures in Kazakhstan designed to take advantage of tax treaties. The advantages conferred by tax treaties can be used by all forms of investment structure in Kazakhstan, including LLPs and JSCs.

4.30 Tax Exemptions on Dividend Payments

[253] Under the Tax Code, dividends paid on the shares will be exempt from tax provided the shares are on the official list of a stock exchange in Kazakhstan (i.e., KASE) at the time the dividend is accrued.

[254] Dividends paid on shares that are not admitted to the official list of the KASE as well as dividends paid on participating interests at the time such dividend is accrued will be exempt from any tax payment, reporting or compliance requirements in Kazakhstan if the following conditions are met simultaneously:

(1) the non-resident shareholder/participant has owned the underlying shares/participating interests or ownership stake in the Kazakhstan company that pays the dividends for more than three years as of the date of the dividend payment;

(2) the non-resident shareholder/participant is not a resident of a country with a favourable tax regime;

(3) the Kazakhstan company that pays the dividends to the non-resident shareholder/participant is not a subsurface user; and

(4) more than 50% of the value of the assets of the Kazakhstan company that pays the dividends is made up of property of entities which are not Kazakhstan subsurface users.

4.31 Tax Exemptions on Capital Gain Income

[255] The tax relief on capital gain income resulting from a sale of shares/participating interests is discussed above in the section '*Capital Gain Tax Exemption*'.

4.32 Debt Financing

[256] Finance costs associated with the acquisition of shares/participating interests by a Kazakhstan company will not be deductible for corporate tax purposes in Kazakhstan (unless the acquisition of shares/interests in other companies is the main activity of such Kazakhstan company). Finance costs incurred by a foreign company associated with the acquisition of shares/interests in a Kazakhstan company will be subject to the taxation rules of the country where such foreign company is resident.

4.33 Thin Capitalization

[257] The 'thin capitalization' rule in Kazakhstan applies to a loan between a Kazakhstan company and its lender (including to a loan between a Kazakhstan company and its foreign shareholder/participant) for purposes of the deductibility of a certain portion of interest by a Kazakhstan company for CIT purposes.

[258] Generally, interest payments will be deductible in full for the CIT purposes only where the debt-to-equity ratio does not exceed four-to-one (or seven-to-one for financial organizations, except for microfinancing organizations). Interest paid on a loan in excess of these debt-to-equity ratios is not deductible for CIT purposes.

4.34 Transfer Pricing

[259] In Kazakhstan, transfer pricing matters are regulated mainly by the Transfer Pricing Law,[27] which came into effect on 1 January 2009.

[260] Under the Transfer Pricing Law, the following types of cross-border transactions are subject to transfer pricing control:

(1) export and import of goods;
(2) transactions related to the provision of works and services where the counterparty to the transaction is a non-resident without a registered PE in Kazakhstan;
(3) transactions between Kazakhstan residents relating to the sale and purchase of goods, provision of works and services, concluded abroad.

[261] In-country transactions can also be subject to transfer pricing control if they are related to cross-border transactions and:

(1) the Kazakhstan party to a transaction related to the sale of minerals is a subsurface user; or
(2) either party to the transaction is enjoying a tax holiday; or
(3) either party to the transaction had tax losses during the two years preceding the transaction.

[262] In general, the scope of transactions which are potentially subject to transfer pricing control is extremely broad. One of the rules which determine the interrelationship between the parties to a transaction states that a transaction where the price deviates from the market price is a transaction performed between related parties. This provision allows the Kazakhstan tax and customs authorities to treat any transaction with a price deviating from the market as a related party transaction.

[263] To avoid a transfer price adjustment, cross-border transactions should be on an arm's-length basis. The Transfer Pricing Law does not specify any particular tolerance or threshold for a deviation from the market price which will trigger a transfer price adjustment. Hence, a transfer price adjustment may potentially apply if the transaction price deviates from the market price by any amount. As a result, the Kazakhstan tax and customs authorities have excessive rights in determining 'related parties' and 'market prices' which allow them to adjust prices resulting in an additional assessment of taxes, including CIT, VAT and customs payments.

[264] Based on our practical experience, the types of transactions which are mostly exposed to risk from a Transfer Pricing Law perspective are those related to subsurface use operations (export of hydrocarbons and other commodities) and financial services (loans).

---

[27] Law of the Republic of Kazakhstan 'On Transfer Pricing' No. 67-IV dated 5 Jul. 2008 as amended (the *Transfer Pricing Law*).

5 EMPLOYMENT CONSIDERATIONS

5.1 Legislative Framework

[265] The Labour Code[28] is the primary legislation affecting labour and employment in Kazakhstan. Other important laws in this area include the Employment Law,[29] which sets out the general framework for employment policy in Kazakhstan, and the Trade Unions Law,[30] which sets out the legal status and the activity of trade unions. The Work Permit Rules[31] is an important piece of subordinate legislation which regulates work permits for foreign citizens.

5.2 Employment Protection

[266] The Labour Code, which became effective as of 1 January 2016, was adopted in place of the previous labour code. In comparison with the old labour code, which was employee-friendly and which contained numerous protections for employees, a large role in the new Labour Code has been given to collective and contractual relations, aimed at protecting the rights not only of employees but also of employers. The Labour Code does not provide any specific employment protections to employees in the context of an acquisition. In particular, the Labour Code does not contain any provisions entitling employees to management representation or obligations of information or consultation in connection with an acquisition of the business. However, the Labour Code provides that employment can only be terminated for specific reasons as set out in the Code, which includes redundancy. As a result, when acquiring a business in Kazakhstan a new owner generally would not be able to terminate employees at will.

[267] Kazakhstan law provides for the protection of employees through trade unions and collective agreements. However, in practice, trade unions are not very common and mostly exist in large, industrial type enterprises. Trade unions are not particularly influential, except in a few cases where trade unions have a historically strong position inherited from the Soviet times. Collective agreements are common in large enterprises, though they can be used in enterprises where employees are not organized in trade unions.

---

28 Labour Code of the Republic of Kazakhstan No. 414-V dated 23 Nov. 2015, as amended (the *Labour Code*).

29 Law of the Republic of Kazakhstan 'On Employment of the Population' No. 482-V dated 6 Apr. 2016, as amended (the *Employment Law*).

30 Law of the Republic of Kazakhstan 'On Trade Unions' No. 211-V dated 27 Jun. 2014 (the *Trade Unions Law*).

31 Rules and Conditions on Issuance and/or Extension of Work Permits to Employers for Attraction of Foreign Labour Force, as well as Performance of Intra-corporate Transfer, approved by the Order of the Acting Minister of Health Care and Social Development of the Kazakhstan Government No. 559 dated 27 Jun. 2016, as amended (the *Work Permit Rules*).

[268] Trade unions and collective agreements mostly focus on general employment rights and conditions (such as working hours, vacations, benefits, health and safety matters). Trade unions can play an important role in cases of staff reductions, in particular where they are given the right to be consulted on the termination of employees. Otherwise, trade unions and collective agreements rarely (if at all) deal with matters directly related to acquisitions.

[269] The previous labour code contained a provision that in the event of a change of participants or shareholders of the employer, a collective agreement continues to be in force for three months after such change. Upon the expiry of the three month period, the parties may replace, amend or retain the existing collective agreement. The current Labour Code eliminates this provision, providing instead for administrative liability for evading participation in negotiations on entering into, amending or supplementing the collective agreement, or unreasonably refusing to conclude a collective agreement.

[270] Individual employment agreements may only be terminated based on grounds set out in the Labour Code. These grounds include, but are not limited to, termination upon:

    (1) mutual agreement;
    (2) expiry of the employment contract;
    (3) liquidation of the employer;
    (4) staff reduction (redundancy);
    (5) relocation of the employer where the employee refuses to be transferred to another location; and
    (6) persistent or repeated misconduct or a single, serious act of misconduct (such as misconduct committed during business hours under the influence of alcohol, drugs or other forms of intoxication).

[271] Exceptions from this provision (allowing termination only on specific grounds) are permitted for certain types of employees, such as the CEO of a legal entity. A CEO can be dismissed without cause based on a resolution of the owner of the company.

[272] The legislation establishes a minimum monthly salary (currently KZT42 500 or approximately USD99) and salaries cannot be lower than this minimum amount. Working conditions vary depending on the sector.

[273] Typically, other than in very large organizations, trade unions are not a major factor in relations with employees or in determining compensation.

5.3 Pensions

[274] The Pensions Law[32] provides for a fully funded, defined contribution pension system which requires each employed individual to make contributions to his individual account with the state-owned pension fund. For more detailed information with respect to the amounts of contributions to the pension fund, please refer to the section '*Taxation Aspects*' above.

As a general rule, the retirement age is 63 for men and 60 for women. It is expected that the female retirement age will be gradually raised up to 63 in 2027.

5.4 Retention of Key Management and Employees

[275] The law does not provide any mechanism to ensure the continuation of individual vendors, members of the management team or other key employees. By law, employees have a right to terminate their employment by giving thirty days' notice unless otherwise agreed. Therefore, retention strategies used in an acquisition context are typically in the form of contractual undertakings.

[276] Non-competition clauses are often imposed on vendors and key employees in the context of acquisitions. Moreover, the Labour Code introduced an option for an employer to enter into a non-competition agreement with its employees. However, the enforcement of such agreements in Kazakhstan courts is inconsistent and therefore there is no established judicial practice in this regard.

5.5 Treatment of Foreign Employees

[277] Generally, there are no restrictions on foreign managers or directors for foreign or local companies in Kazakhstan. However, it should be noted that in order to be able to hire a foreign citizen, a company must obtain a work permit from the relevant local authority. Pursuant to the Work Permit Rules, issuance of work permits and their effectiveness is subject to compliance by the employer with the following ratio requirements: (i) 70% of employees in the first category (i.e., CEO s and their deputies) and in the second category (i.e., heads of divisions) must be citizens of Kazakhstan, and (ii) 90% of employees in the third and fourth categories (i.e., other qualified specialists and workers) must be citizens of Kazakhstan. The quota requirement does not apply to entities that are participants of an SEZ with a project value of more than 1 000 000 MSI (KZT2 917 000 000 or approximately USD6 783 720), as well as its subcontractors. It is not required to obtain a work permit for foreign employees in (i) Astana Hub and its participants that are top managers and specialists with higher education; (ii) participants of the AIFC and AIFC bodies.

---

[32] Law of the Republic of Kazakhstan 'On Pension Provision in the Republic of Kazakhstan' No. 105-V dated 21 Jun. 2013, as amended (the *Pensions Law*).

[278] As noted above, in order to be able to hire a foreign citizen, the company must obtain a work permit from the relevant local authority. The work permit requirement applies to citizens of all jurisdictions, (except for citizens of the Republic of Belarus, the Russian Federation, the Republic of Armenia and the Kyrgyz Republic, which are part of the common economic zone), and also to foreign citizens having a residence permit.

[279] There are certain exceptions from the work permit requirement. These exceptions apply in particular to heads of branches and representative offices of foreign legal entities, CEOs and deputy CEOs of Kazakhstan legal entities wholly owned by foreign individuals/legal entities, employees engaged by the participants and corporate bodies of the AIFC or by Astana Hub or its participants, chief executives of legal entities that have entered into an investment contract with the Kazakhstan Government worth USD50m or more, and chief executives of legal entities investing in priority sectors of the economy through a contract with the authorized state body on investments.

[280] Work permits are granted based on quotas that are distributed among the regions and the cities of Almaty, Shymkent and Nur-Sultan (former Astana). The Ministry of Labor and Social Protection of the Population of Kazakhstan sets the quota annually following an assessment of the local job markets and of the availability of skilled Kazakhstan personnel to fill vacant positions.

[281] Following submission of an application by the employer, the decision on whether or not to grant a work permit should be adopted by the local authority within seven working days. However, if granted, in practice it takes longer (usually up to 1.5–2 months) to receive the issued work permit. The timeframe varies because it requires the local authority to issue a notification on the adopted decision and following receipt of such notification by the employer, the latter must pay the duty (the amount of which varies depending on the sector of the economy in which the relevant employee will work) and must provide payment documents to the local authority.

[282] In addition to the work permit, in order to be able to enter and remain in Kazakhstan citizens of most jurisdictions are required to obtain a visa.

[283] A work visa can be issued on the basis of a work permit and for the duration of the work permit. A work visa is granted within five working days unless more time is required to review the application. In this case, the review process increases up to thirty calendar days.

[284] Applications for a residence permit are reviewed within seventeen calendar days but in practice almost always take more time.

[285] The obtaining of visas or residence permits requires payment of consular fees and state duties, respectively. Many companies use intermediaries to help obtain work permits or residence cards. The fees of such intermediaries can range up to several thousand dollars for each permit they help obtain.

[286] Generally, it is not an onerous responsibility to be a director of a company in Kazakhstan. In terms of the level of responsibility, in practice, the chief executive has the primary responsibility. Members of a board or a supervisory council are also subject to liability for their actions (or failure to act), though the legislation in this respect is still relatively new and in practice, the standard of responsibility for such persons is lower than that of a chief executive. It is possible to insure the director's liability in Kazakhstan.

6 ACCOUNTING TREATMENT

[287] The general requirements as to the format and content of group accounts are set out in the Accounting Law.[33] Depending on the category of the legal entity, the Accounting Law requires legal entities to apply either national reporting standards (pursuant to the National Accounting Standards approved by the Order of the Minister of Finance of the Republic of Kazakhstan dated 31 January 2013) or IFRS. The categories of a legal entity are based on turnover and the number of employees. 'Small businesses' must apply national standards. 'Medium businesses' must apply IFRS for small and medium businesses. 'Large businesses' and 'companies of public interest' (such as financial organizations, subsurface users, JSCs and companies in state ownership) must apply IFRS. Therefore, in the context of a business combination, Kazakhstan legal entities would most likely be subject to IFRS and, consequently, from an accounting perspective the treatment of such business combination would not be materially different from the treatment of an analogous combination in another jurisdiction where IFRS also applies.

7 FUTURE DEVELOPMENTS

[288] M&A activity in Kazakhstan in 2017–2021 has been diverse and included activity in various sectors, including oil & gas, mining, banking, telecommunications, retail and other sectors. We note that during this period there was a particularly high level of M&A activity in the banking sector due to financial instability experienced by the local banks (e.g., acquisition of Kazkommertsbank JSC by Halyk Bank JSC, acquisition of ATFBank JSC by First Heartland Jysan Bank JSC) and significant support provided by the state. We expect that implementation of the programme launched by the NBK to improve the financial stability of banks could spur further M&A activity in the banking sector over the next few years.

[289] We note that the introduction of a free-floating exchange rate for the Kazakhstan currency (Tenge) on 20 August 2015 negatively affected M&A activity in the retail sector and other import-oriented businesses. In our view, the consequences of a floating exchange rate regime will continue to affect M&A activity in these sectors in the near future.

---

[33] Law of the Republic of Kazakhstan 'On Accounting and Financial Reporting' No. 234-III dated 28 Feb. 2007, as amended (the *Accounting Law*).

[290] We expect that a number of government initiatives could potentially act as catalysts of further M&A activity in Kazakhstan during the next few years. These initiatives include the following:

- a comprehensive privatization programme designed to reduce state involvement in the economy by way of sale of various assets of the Samruk-Kazyna group and state-owned enterprises in 2021–2025, as approved on 29 December 2020;
- a new Tax Code aimed at, among other objectives, better administration of taxation and improvement of the investment climate. The new Tax Code was approved on 25 December 2018 and, except for certain of its provisions, came into force on 1 January 2018; and
- establishment of the AIFC operating within a special legal regime based on English Law and providing its members with a preferential tax regime, simplified currency control, beneficial visa and employment regimes, simplified registration processes and services of its own independent financial and arbitration courts.

[291] We note that the general push by the Kazakhstan Government in 2015–2017 to improve the investment climate has resulted in a number of positive legislative changes that improve the climate for acquisition activity in Kazakhstan.

Contents

Kinstellar

Kinstellar is a leading independent law firm in Emerging Europe, Turkey and Central Asia, with offices in Almaty and Nur-Sultan (Kazakhstan), Belgrade (Serbia), Bratislava (Slovakia), Bucharest (Romania), Budapest (Hungary), Istanbul (Turkey), Kyiv (Ukraine), Prague (the Czech Republic) and Sofia (Bulgaria).

Kinstellar's clients include leading international and regional corporations, banks and other financial institutions, state bodies, multi-lateral institutions, and international law firms with clients that require top-quality legal counsel in our jurisdictions. Kinstellar handles the most important and complex assignments for clients across diverse industries and business sectors.

Authors

Joel Benjamin is the Managing Partner of the Central Asia practice of Kinstellar. Joel advises international and local clients in various industries, including oil and gas, mining, banking, telecommunications and media. Joel has a broad experience in corporate and commercial transactions with a particular specialism in banking and finance, where he has developed top rankings within Kazakhstan and Central Asia. He has played a leading role in numerous transactions, including bilateral and syndicated loans, trade finance, project finance, equity/debt capital markets and banking matters. Joel has built a strong corporate practice, including work on numerous M&A transactions across sectors, including oil and gas, mining, telecommunications and banking. In addition to Kazakh law expertise, Joel has more than twenty years of experience assisting clients on Uzbekistan law issues.

Joel comes highly recommended by Legal 500, Chambers Global, IFLR 1000, Who's Who Legal and Best Lawyers in Kazakhstan.

Muborak Kambarova is a Counsel in the Tashkent office of Kinstellar. Muborak has twenty years of experience advising international clients investing in Uzbekistan, guiding them in matters of local law and business practice and assisting them in negotiations with government agencies and institutions. She enjoys a solid reputation among clients and peers and has extensive experience handling cross-border transactions and a wide variety of corporate matters, including mergers and acquisitions. Her expertise covers banking and finance as well as mining and the oil and gas sectors. Muborak is listed as one of the country's top lawyers by the leading legal international directories Chambers Global, Legal 500 and IFLR 1000.

List of Abbreviations

Agency	The Agency for External Labour Migration under the Ministry of Labour and Social Protection
Antimonopoly authority	The State Committee of Uzbekistan for Assistance to Privatised Enterprises and Development of Competition;
BCR	Basic Calculation Rate which is set at 245,000 from 1 February 2021 (approximately equal to USD 23.07 as of 26 July 2021);
CBU	The Central Bank of the Republic of Uzbekistan
CIS	Commonwealth of Independent States
Commission	Interdepartmental Commission for Combating Corruption
DTT	Double Taxation Treaty
FEZ	Free Industrial Economic Zones
FLE	Foreign Legal Entity
Foreign Participant	Foreign individual and / or foreign legal entity
Labour Code	The Labour Code of Uzbekistan (No. 161-1 as of 21 December 1995, as amended);
JSC	Joint Stock Company;
LLC	Limited Liability Company;
M&A	Mergers and Acquisitions;
MMW	the Monthly Minimum Wage, which is set at UZS 747,300 from 1 February 2021 (approximately equal to USD 70.40 as of 26 July 2021);
NAS	National Accounting Standards of Uzbekistan;
PE	Permanent Establishment;
Privatisation law	Law 'On Denationalization and Privatisation'
PSA	Production Sharing Agreement (the Law on Production Sharing Agreements No. 312-II as of 7 December 2011);

SIZ	Special Industrial Zones
SME	Small and Medium Enterprises
Special Commission	Commission prescribed by Law 'On the Approval of Some Administrative Regulations for Providing Public Services in the Sphere of Antimonopoly Regulation in Commodity and Financial Market' No. 338 dated 28 May 2020
State Assets Management Agency	State Assets Management Agency of the Republic of Uzbekistan
Uzbekistan	The Republic of Uzbekistan.
UZS	Uzbekistan Soum or Som (the currency of Uzbekistan). On 26 July 2021, the exchange rate is USD 1 = UZS 10 635);

1 LOCAL ECONOMIC, POLITICAL AND CULTURAL ASPECTS

1.1 General Comments on the Country Profile

[01] Uzbekistan is located in the heart of Central Asia. It lies mainly between two major rivers – the Syr Darya (ancient Jaxartes River) to the northeast and the Amu Darya (ancient Oxus River) to the southwest, though they only partly form its boundaries. Uzbekistan is bordered by five neighbouring countries: Kazakhstan to the northwest, Kyrgyzstan and Tajikistan to the southeast, Afghanistan to the south, and Turkmenistan to the southwest.

[02] Uzbekistan has a diverse culture and many languages. The official language is Uzbek, which uses a Latin alphabet. Approximately 85% of the population speaks Uzbek. Use of the Russian language is widespread in the Uzbek capital, Tashkent. The *soum* (UZS) is the national currency.

[03] The total population of the country is around 34.6[1] m people. The capital city, Tashkent, has a population of about 2.4 m people. The country is ethnically diverse: Uzbeks comprise around 81% of the population, Russians (5.4%), Tajiks (4.0%), Kazakhs (3.0%), and others (6.5%).

[04] Uzbekistan's natural resources include petroleum, natural gas, gold, silver, uranium, molybdenum, tungsten, coal, copper, zinc, and lead. The country has large mineral reserves of uranium, copper, and gold.

[05] Uzbekistan is famous for its cotton industry and is the sixth-largest producer of cotton and fifth-largest exporter of cotton in the world. Uzbekistan is one of the largest exporters of gold and of natural gas.

[06] Uzbekistan inherited a good network of roads and railways from the Soviet era. Over the past decade, the government has been actively attracting financing to improve the existing national network of roads and to construct new roads. High-speed trains link the capital, Tashkent, with the cities of Samarkand and Bukhara. It is easy and safe to travel between cities by car, train or aeroplane.

1.2 Legal System

[07] The legal system of Uzbekistan is based on a civil law system. It is based on written sources of law, namely the Constitution of Uzbekistan, constitutional laws, codes, laws, presidential decrees, decrees of the Cabinet of Ministers, and other normative legal acts.

[08] In general, depending on the qualification of the judge and complexity of the case, laws are enforced relatively efficiently. The court process itself is considered to

---

[1] According to the State Committee of the Republic of Uzbekistan on statistics – as of 1 Apr. 2021, preliminary data.

be time-consuming. Any administrative, civil, economic or criminal case can go through several stages of consideration in the courts. The judicial system is three-tiered, and only a limited number of cases go to the third tier.

[09] The identification of assets for acquisition in Uzbekistan is becoming easier these days. The government has announced an ambitious plan to reform the country's economy, including through privatisation of a significant portion of state assets and by attracting foreign investment into the local economy. According to the PKM No. 166, 75% of state-owned enterprises will be available for privatisation.[2] Among those to be partially privatised are Uzbekneftegaz, (which contributes 15%of the country's GDP), Navoi Mining and Metallurgical Combine, Uzbekistan Airways, Uzbekistan Railways, and car maker Uzavtosanoat.

[10] The government under an e-government programme has introduced electronic online auctions on a single electronic trading platform 'E-IJRO AUKSION' (www.e-auksion.uz). Pursuant to PP-3149 auctions for the sale of property in the execution of judicial acts and acts of other bodies are carried out exclusively on E-IJRO AUKSION platform.[3]

[11] The government has introduced the single portal of interactive government services, my.gov.uz. through which Individuals and legal entities can obtain a wide spectrum of government services online.

[12] Despite numerous ongoing efforts by the government to simplify the legislative framework for doing business and attracting foreign investors, acquisitions in Uzbekistan may still be difficult to carry out. To facilitate acquisitions, investors may seek assistance from law firms, consultants or responsible government agencies, which will help them in structuring and setting up a business.

[13] Generally, acquisitions in Uzbekistan can be performed through the acquisition of shares/ participatory interests in an existing company from either the state or a private shareholder.

1.3 Current Economic Aspects

[14] COVID-19 pandemic significantly affected economic development of the state, especially in the first half of 2020. A sizable portion of international support and timely containment allowed to effectively respond and prevent significant economic drop.

---

[2] Decree of Cabinet of Ministers 'On Approval of the Strategy of Management and Reform of Enterprises with State Participation for 2021-2021' No. 166 dated 29 Mar. 2021.

[3] Decree of the President of the Republic of Uzbekistan 'On the Measures for Regular Improvement of Procedures for Sale of Property in the Execution of Judicial Acts and Acts of Other Bodies' PP-3149 dated 27 Jul. 2017.

[15] In 2020, Uzbek GDP reached 580.20 trillion Uzbekistan Sums (UZS) which equates to approximately USD 55 076 877 480 bn.[4] It is 1.6% higher than in 2019. Generally, the growth rate of real GDP for 2017–2019 is 5.2%.[5] However, due to the current pandemic, growth rate fell to its lowest level for the first time, which is 1.6%. According to the World Bank forecast, GDP growth rate in Uzbekistan will reach 4.8% in 2021.[6]

[16] The IMF forecasts that annual GDP growth of the Uzbek economy in 2021 will be 5% and that by 2022 annual GDP growth will reach 5.3%.[7]

[17] The IMF expects inflation to decrease below 10% in 2021.[8] The CBU aims to reduce inflation to 5% by 2023.

[18] The current account balance of Uzbekistan was negative 5.4% of GDP in 2020. According to the IMF forecast, the figure will be negative 6.4% of GDP in 2021 and is expected to be negative 5.9 GDP in 2022.

[19] Until recently, there were not many M&A transactions taking place in the country, and there are no published details of deal volumes and payment types concerning M&A transactions.

1.4 Main Industries

[20] Key industries in Uzbekistan include the oil and gas, mining, textile, mechanical engineering, petrochemical, metalworking, forestry, pulp and paper, agriculture, chemical and food industries.[9] In 2020, Uzbekistan was the world's sixth-largest producer and third-largest exporter of cotton and the ninth-largest producer of gold.[10]

[21] Article 4 of the Privatisation Law and the Presidential Decree 'On Measures for Further Improvement of the Procedures for the Implementation of Public Property Objects' No. PP-3067 dated 16 June 2017 sets out the list of strategic objects whose ownership rests exclusively with the state and which cannot be privatised under the applicable law, including:

- land (except for cases provided by the applicable law), subsoil, inland waters, the air basin, and flora and fauna within the territory of the Republic of Uzbekistan;

---

[4] *See* more in https://stat.uz/ru/press-tsentr/novosti-goskomstata/7509-proizvodstvo-valovogo-vnutren nego-produkta-yanvar-dekabr-2020-goda-2 Report on GDP of Uzbekistan in 2020.

[5] See more in https://stat.uz/ru/press-tsentr/novosti-goskomstata/7851-o-zbekistonda-yil-boshidan-buyon-yalpi-ichki-mahsulot-hajmi-necha-foizga-o-sdi-2.

[6] World Bank. 2021. *Europe and Central Asia Economic Update, Spring 2021: Data, Digitalization, and Governance*. Washington, DC: World Bank https://openknowledge.worldbank.org/handle/10986/35273

[7] IMF, '2021 Article IV Consultation-Press Release; and Staff Report' (IMF 2021).

[8] *Ibid.*

[9] Industry of Uzbekistan (State Committee of the Republic of Uzbekistan on Statistics 2020).

[10] Statista.com.

- objects of cultural heritage, including museums and protected natural habitat;
- properties of bodies of state power and the administration of the Republic of Uzbekistan;
- funds of the state budget of the Republic of Uzbekistan, state foreign exchange reserves, state special purpose funds, funds of the Central Bank of the Republic of Uzbekistan, as well as the gold reserves of the Republic of Uzbekistan; and
- properties of the Armed Forces of the Republic of Uzbekistan, the State Security Service of the Republic of Uzbekistan and the Ministry of Internal Affairs of the Republic of Uzbekistan.

[22] Since its independence in 1991, Uzbekistan's major assets have been controlled by the state. This situation is changing at the moment with a new president having been elected in 2016. The President signed a Decree 'On Measures for Accelerated Reformation of Enterprises with the Participation of the State and Privatisation of State Assets' UP-6096 dated 27 October 2020. According to the Decree over 620 state assets have been transformed, put up for public auction, sold to the private sector and selling state assets at a *zero*-redemption value has been cancelled. In addition, UP-6167 'On Measure for Further Accelerating Processes of Privatisation of State Assets' dated 11 February 2021 was adopted to accelerate privatisation process.

[23] In the past, the buyers in M&A transactions in Uzbekistan were mainly corporate buyers and there was not much interest from financial investors.

1.5 Cultural Aspects

[24] Uzbekistan is in the midst of rapid political and economic changes that are mainly focused on improving the business environment and attracting FDI to the country, as well as maintaining geopolitical stability and geo-economic integration in Central Asia. Several normative legal acts such as the Resolution of the Cabinet of Ministers 'On Organisation of Work of the Agency of Attracting Foreign Investments under the Ministry of Investments and Foreign Trade of the Republic of Uzbekistan' dated 24 July 2019, Law No. ZRU-598 'On Investments and Investment Activities' dated 25 December 2019, Law No. ZRU-674 'On International Commercial Arbitration' dated 16 February 2021 have been adopted in order to create more favourable conditions for investors. It is expected that the number of foreign companies will rise in the coming years, as the country becomes more attractive for doing business.

[25] Legislative reforms are currently being implemented to reduce the barriers and restrictions on doing business and to simplify the conduct of business and reporting procedures. Therefore, the President signed Decree No. UP-6191 'On Additional Measures for further Creation of Favorable Conditions for the Population and Business when Using State Services, Reduction of Bureaucratic Barriers'

dated 23 march 2021. Such reforms are creating many opportunities to open new business areas for foreign investors.

[26] The overall business climate may be described as stable, with potential growth in the form of more radical reforms toward a market economy. Currently, more than 11,781 enterprises with foreign investments operate in Uzbekistan,[11] including LG, Lukoil, British-American Tobacco and many others.

[27] The role of small business and private entrepreneurship is also increasing in Uzbekistan. The government recognises the importance of the SME business community for the economy and has been updating legislation to reduce the tax and administrative burden on small businesses. During the pandemic, the government passed several legislations on supporting SMEs. The Presidential Decree PP-5087 'On Additional Measure to Improve the Entrepreneurship Support System, Further Improve the Business Climate' dated 21 April 2021 introduced new measures to support SME and other entrepreneurs.

[28] Uzbekistan is not a liberal place to do business, as legislation strictly regulates each aspect of doing business.

[29] Although labour costs are not very expensive, Uzbekistan is not a cheap place to do business. The cost of doing business may vary from region to region and depends heavily on the particular sphere of business, employment costs (including taxes), etc. Transportation costs may be a significant cost of business.

[30] In addition, the country is rich in natural resources, with more than 100 types of mineral resources, including significant deposits of natural gas, uranium, silver, copper, and other rare metals.

[31] It is normal in Uzbekistan to bring a gift when you visit someone, either socially or in a business context.

2 THE REGULATORY FRAMEWORK

2.1 Business Vehicles

[32] The most common form of corporate vehicle used by foreign companies in Uzbekistan is the Limited Liability Company (LLC). An LLC is a commercial entity that can be created either by an individual or legal entity, both by Uzbek nationals or foreigners.[12]

---

[11] As of 1 Jan. 2021. Cited in https://www.stat.uz/en/press-center/news-of-committee/7277-hududlarda-xorijiy-kapital-ishtirokida-faoliyat-ko-rsatayotgan-korxonalar-soni-qancha-3.

[12] According to Art. 3 of the Law 'On Companies with Limited and Additional Liability' No. 310-II dated 6 Dec. 2001, it is stated that 'LLC members are not liable for its obligations or to bear the risk of losses associated with the activities of the company, within the limits of the value of their contributions'.

Art. 14 of this law states that the minimum amount of statutory fund (charter capital) of the company can be determined in the licensing requirements. The share can be formed both in the form of cash funds, and in the form of property. Further, in the same place:

[33] We note that the LLC with foreign investment might be incorporated in three forms:

    (i) as an ordinary LLC (LLC) – in case if the LLC's charter capital is less than UZS 400,000,000;

   (ii) LLC in the form of the foreign enterprise (FE LLC) – in case if the LLC's charter capital is at least UZS 400,000,000 and all LLC's participatory interest completely belongs to the Foreign Participant(s);[13]

  (iii) LLC in the form of the joint venture (JV LLC) – in case if the LLC's charter capital is at least UZS 400'000'000 and the proportion of participatory interest that belongs to the Foreign Participant(s) is at least 15%.[14]

It is important to note that neither the size of the LLC's charter capital nor the presence of the foreign participant(s) in practice does not grant any incentive or benefit to the LLC.

[34] The process of LLC's incorporation takes place at the regional/district Centre of the Public Services under the Ministry of Justice of the Republic of Uzbekistan depending on the postal address of the enterprise.

[35] Below is a brief summary of an LLC's activities:

	Limited Liability Company
Registration	An LLC must be registered as an Uzbek legal entity with the state registration authority.
Minimum charter capital	No minimum charter capital requirement, except the licensed types of economic activities.
Rental of office space	There is no a statutory requirement for LLC to have an office. An LLC may exist at the postal address. If it is necessary, LLC can rent office space.
Opening of bank accounts	An LLC can open bank accounts in foreign and national currencies and conduct banking transactions.

Art. 15. The contribution to the charter capital of a company may be money, securities, other things, property rights, or other alienable rights having a monetary value.

Art. 16. An increase in the authorized capital of a company is carried out by a decision of the general meeting of the company's participants, adopted by a majority of at least two-thirds of the votes of the total number of votes of the company's participants, if the need for a larger number of votes for making such a decision is not provided for by the charter of the company.

The increase in the charter capital of a company may be carried out at the expense of the property of the company and (or) at the expense of additional contributions of the participants in the company, and (or), if this is not prohibited by the charter of the company, at the expense of contributions of third parties accepted into the company.

13 The Presidential Decree UP-5495 'On Measures for cardinal improvement of the investment climate in the Republic of Uzbekistan' dated 1 Aug. 2018.

14 *Ibid.*

Limited Liability Company

Conducting commercial activities	An LLC may engage in any activity allowed by Uzbek legislation. However, LLC must obtain licences/permits where required by the Licensing Law.[15]
Hiring Uzbek employees	An LLC is able to hire employees in Uzbekistan.
Hiring Foreign employees	An LLC is able to hire foreign employees only after obtaining a permit for employing foreign labour from the local department of the Ministry of Labour. The number of foreign employees is limited by that permit.
Logistical Support	An LLC is able to provide logistical support services such as invitations for personnel, secretarial support, drivers, etc.
Payment for services provided by the Uzbek legal entities	An LLC must pay local service providers in the local currency.
Currency conversion	An LLC is able to apply for the conversion of local currency into foreign currency through a servicing bank.

[36] Under Uzbek legislation, a director is empowered to manage the day-to-day activities of the company. The director is appointed by a decision of the founders of the company. The director may delegate his/her powers to another person under a Power of Attorney.

3 LAWS AFFECTING M&A

[37] In Uzbekistan, the main laws regulating M&A activities are the Civil Code,[16] the law on JSCs,[17] the Law on a Company with Limited and Additional Liability[18] and the Law on Competition.[19] Additionally, the law on the Securities Market[20] and

---

[15] Law of the Republic of Uzbekistan No. 71-II 'Licensing of certain activities', dated 25 May 2000.
[16] The Civil Code (General Part) No. 163-I dated 21 Dec. 1995 and the Civil Code (Special Part) No. 256-I dated 29 Jul. 1996.
[17] Law of the Republic of Uzbekistan No. ZRU-30 dated 6 May 2014.
[18] Law of the Republic of Uzbekistan No. 310-II dated 6 Dec. 2001.
[19] Law of the Republic of Uzbekistan No. ZRU-319 dated 6 Jan. 2012.
[20] Law of the Republic of Uzbekistan No. ZRU-387 dated 3 Jun. 2015.

Rules on Issuance of Securities and State Registration of Issuance of Equity Securities[21] apply to M&A activities in Uzbekistan.

[38] The LLC law applies to the acquisition of a participating interest in an LLC, as well as to the combination and division of an LLC.

[39] If acquisition involves shares in a JSC, the legislation governing JSCs will apply. Transactions involving shares are subject to approval/registration with the State Assets Management Agency and the depository of securities.[22] Government approval may be required to acquire a stake in a state-owned company.

[40] The concept of hostile transactions does not exist in Uzbek law. Therefore, local legislation does not specify any specific requirement for such transactions.

[41] Under Uzbek laws and regulations, the main method of conducting M&A transactions is to acquire a stake in an existing company through a share sale/purchase agreement.[23]

[42] Local law allows for the reorganisation of a company, but in practice, this is rare. Under Uzbek legislation, there are no voluntary codes, guidelines or self-regulating mechanisms concerning M&A transactions.

4 RELEVANT REGULATORY AUTHORITIES

[43] The Cabinet of Ministers, the Ministry of Justice, the CBU, the Antimonopoly Committee, and the State Assets Management Agency are the main regulatory agencies that have jurisdiction over M&A transactions.

[44] The Cabinet of Ministers is responsible for making decisions on the merger of state-owned legal entities. It has the power to grant consent for the merger of surviving and dissolving companies.

[45] The Antimonopoly Committee and the State Assets Management Agency are responsible for antimonopoly clearance and, in certain cases, for the pre-approval of mergers as required by the Competition Law.

[46] The Ministry of Justice and its relevant regional departments are responsible for the registration of reorganised legal entities.

[47] If the M&A transaction involves the merger of banks, consent from both the Cabinet of Ministers and Central Bank is required.

---

[21] Adopted by the order of the general director of the Centre for Coordination and Control of Securities Market under the State Property Committee of Uzbekistan (registered with the Ministry of Justice No. 2000 dated 30 Aug. 2009.

[22] Law on the Organization of the Activity of the Agency for Managing State Assets of the Republic of Uzbekistan No. PP-4112 dated 14 Jan. 2019.

[23] Note: Some transactions connected with share purchase agreements are subject to the Competition Law.

[48] Uzbekistan's legal-normative acts and regulations specify the timing implications for different government consents and licences. These depend on the type of consent or licence required. For example, the period for consideration by the registering body of documents submitted for state registration of the issue of securities must not exceed thirty days from the date of their receipt by the registering body. During this period, the registering body is obliged to carry out the state registration of the issue of securities or to make a reasoned decision to refuse the state registration of such issue.[24] In practice, however, obtaining approvals for an M&A transaction may take longer. It is possible to engage independently with regulatory bodies, but generally legal entities and foreign investors hire professional advisors to carry out the whole process of the transaction.

5 CONTROLS/RESTRICTIONS ON FOREIGN INVESTMENT

[49] As stated earlier, Article 4 of the Privatisation Law and the Presidential Decree 'On Measures for the Further Improvement of the Procedures for the Implementation of Public Property Objects' No. PP-3067 dated 16 June 2017 sets out the list of strategic objects whose ownership rests exclusively with the state and which cannot be privatised under the applicable law, including (but not limited to):

- land (except for cases provided by applicable law), subsoil, inland waters, air basin, flora and fauna within the territory of the Republic of Uzbekistan;
- objects of cultural heritage, including museums and protected natural habitat;
- properties of bodies of state power and administration of the Republic of Uzbekistan;
- state television, radio reception and radio broadcasting enterprises; and
- funds of the state budget of the Republic of Uzbekistan, state foreign exchange reserves, state special purpose funds, the funds of the Central Bank of the Republic of Uzbekistan, as well as the gold reserves of the Republic of Uzbekistan.

[50] Other than the list referred to above, a foreign purchaser may acquire a 100% interest in an Uzbek legal entity and the law does not establish any threshold for domestic ownership or any restrictions on foreign ownership.

[51] There are no restrictions on foreign directors/managers.

[52] If the company is privately owned, the presence of a governmental official is not required on its supervisory board.

[53] Permits are not required for a foreign-owned company to trade.

---

[24] Article 52 of the Rules 'On Securities Issues and State Registration of Issues of Equity Securities', adopted by the order of the general director of the Centre for Coordination and Control of Securities Market under the State Property Committee of Uzbekistan (registered with the Ministry of Justice No. 2000 dated 30 Aug. 2009).

[54] Land and minerals in the soil are owned by the state. Land can be granted to a foreign-owned company either for temporary or permanent use and depending on the purpose of use, minerals/mining rights can be granted to a foreign-owned company. A foreign-owned company is entitled to own immovable property.

6 INCENTIVES FOR FOREIGN INVESTMENT

6.1 Incentives Available to Foreign Investors

[55] The legal regulations associated with attracting foreign investment to Uzbekistan are as follows:

- Law on Investment and Investment Activities;[25]
- a number of normative and legal acts adopted in the form of decisions of the president and government resolutions.

[56] In accordance with current legislation, the concept of foreign direct investment includes:

- investments by foreign investors of tangible and intangible goods and rights to them, including the right to intellectual property;
- any income from foreign investments invested by foreign investors in the business and other types of activity;
- movable and immovable property;
- intellectual property rights, including patented or non-patented technical, technological, commercial and other knowledge prepared in the form of technical documentations, skills and production experience necessary to organise a particular type of production, as well as other values, not prohibited by the legislation of the Republic of Uzbekistan.[26]

[57] There are no restrictions in Uzbekistan in respect of the forms of business investment vehicles. Foreign investors can create enterprises in the territory of Uzbekistan in any organisational and legal form permitted by law.

6.2 Tax Privileges

[58] Articles 471–476 of the Tax Code[27] and the Presidential Decree No. UP-3594 dated 11 April 2005 stipulate that enterprises in priority economic sectors (as per the list in the Decree) attracting direct private foreign investment are exempt from corporate income tax, property tax, and the unified tax for certain period based on the amount of investment made in accordance with legislation.[28] These tax benefits

---

[25] No. ZRU-598 dated 25 Dec. 2019.
[26] *Ibid.*, Art. 3.
[27] Tax Code of the Republic of Uzbekistan dated 30 Dec. 2019.
[28] Tax Code, Art. 376.

are provided for the volume of private foreign direct investments (from USD 300 000) and are applied on condition that legal entities are located in territories determined by legislation, that FDI is made without state guarantee, that the authorised share capital of the foreign investor is not less than 33% (for a JSC – not less than 15%), that investment is in the form of freely convertible currency or new modern technologies equipment, and reinvestment of 50% of the income received as a result of tax benefits and other obligatory payments for the period of application tax exemption.[29]

[59] These preferences are granted to legal entities from three years up to a ten-year period if the investment is equivalent to:

- from USD300 000 to USD3m – for a period of three years;
- from USD3m to USD10m – for a period of five years;
- more than USD10m – for a period of seven years.[30]

[60] If the investment conditions deteriorate with subsequent legislation, these benefits are valid for the entire period for which they were provided.

[61] Foreign companies enter into production sharing agreements (PSAs) with Uzbekistan in the oil and gas or other sectors related to prospecting, exploration of deposits and mining operations in accordance with the law on PSAs. According to this law, their contractors and subcontractors are also exempt from payment of all types of taxes and other obligatory payments established in Uzbekistan related to the conduct of prospecting and exploration work in the subsoil area. During the term of the agreement, the investor pays taxes and other obligatory payments in accordance with applicable legislation, considering the features stipulated in Article 256 of the Tax Code of Uzbekistan. In particular, tax on profit is paid at the same rates as for residents (12% for 2021), but at the same time, the entire cost of profitable products belonging to the investor is subject to taxation without deduction of expenses.

[62] Goods (works, services) provided by legal entities – residents of Uzbekistan – to investors and (or) operators participating in the performance of work under a PSA are taxed at zero-rate value-added tax.

6.3 Exemptions on Payment of Customs Duties

[63] The following are exempt from payment of customs duties:

- property imported into Uzbekistan by enterprises with foreign investment (where the share of foreign investment in the statutory fund is at least 33%) for their own production needs, within two years from the date of their state registration;

---

[29] *Ibid.*, Art. 377.
[30] The Presidential Decree No. UP-3594 'On additional measures to increase attracting private foreign investment' dated 11 Apr. 2005.

- goods imported by foreign legal entities that have made direct investments in the economy of Uzbekistan total amount of more than USD50m, provided that the imported goods are products of their own production;
- technological equipment imported into the territory of Uzbekistan, according to the list approved in accordance with applicable legislation, as well as their components and spare parts, if this is provided for by the terms of the contract;[31]

[64] Enterprises with foreign investment, along with their associated tax and customs incentives, also enjoy all the same types of tax and customs privileges as are provided to Uzbek legal entities, including in particular those available in the production of export-oriented and import-substituting products; the production of consumer goods subject to increased demand; exports of goods (works, services); the import of technological equipment; the transfer of property as investment obligations; and others.

[65] Article 297 of the Customs Code of Uzbekistan defines the general list of tariff preferences in the form of exemptions from or reduction of customs duty as well as its return.

[66] In addition, under Article 300 of the Customs Code, tariff preferences are granted in the form of an exemption from customs duties, reduction of the rates of customs duties or the establishment of quotas for preferential importation into the customs territory, or the preferential export of goods originating from certain states from this territory.

[67] Customs duties on goods in Uzbekistan are not applied under the following conditions:

- where they originate from and are imported to the customs territory of states forming a free trade zone with Uzbekistan or with which Uzbekistan has established a free trade regime;
- where they originate from Uzbekistan and are exported from its customs territory to states forming a free trade zone with Uzbekistan or with which Uzbekistan has a free trade regime.

[68] For goods originating from states with which Uzbekistan has concluded an international agreement on the establishment of a free trade zone, a resident of a state which is party to a treaty with the customs territory of another Contracting State does not apply customs duties if the goods are exported/imported. A resident means an organisation established in the territory of a state or a natural person permanently residing in the territory of that state. In other cases, the customs duty rate is applied in accordance with the customs tariff.

[69] Regardless of the country of departure of the goods and their exporter, customs duties, at the rates established by the customs tariff, are not applied to goods originating from countries with which Uzbekistan has established most-favoured-nation treatment in trade and economic relations.

---

[31] Customs Code of the Republic of Uzbekistan dated 20 Jan. 2016, Art. 297.

6.4 Free Economic Zones

[70] A number of free industrial economic zones (FEZ) and special industrial zones (SIZ) have been established in Uzbekistan. The operational regime in each FEZ is determined by a specific regulation. Below please find a brief overview of each FEZ. The list of FEZ is provided below:

- Navoi FEZ
- Angren FEZ
- Jizzakh FEZ
- Urgut FEZ
- Gijduvon FEZ
- Kokand FEZ
- Namangan FEZ
- Hazarasp FEZ
- Termez FEZ
- Nukus-pharm FEZ
- Zomin-pharm FEZ
- Kosonsoy-pharm FEZ
- Sirdaryo-pharm FEZ
- Boysun-pharm FEZ
- Parkent-pharm FEZ
- Andijon-pharm FEZ
- Charvak FEZ
- Balik FEZ
- Sirdaryo FEZ
- Bukhoro-agro FEZ
- Chirokchi FEZ.

6.4.1 FEZ 'Navoi' (Presidential Decree No. UP-4059)[32]

[71] According to the Decree of the President of Uzbekistan No. UP-4853 dated 26 October 2016 'On Additional Measures to Activate and Expand the Activities of the Free Economic Zones' enterprises located in FEZ are exempt from payment:

- land tax, income tax, tax on property of legal entities, tax on improvement and development of social infrastructure, single tax payment for micro firms and small enterprises, as well as mandatory contributions to the Republican Road Fund and extra-budgetary Fund for reconstruction, overhaul and equipment of secondary schools, professional colleges, academic lyceums and medical institutions under the Ministry of Finance of the Republic of Uzbekistan;
- customs payments (except for customs clearance fees) for equipment, raw materials and components imported for their own production needs;

---

[32] Dated 2 Dec. 2008.

- customs payments (except for customs clearance fees) for construction materials not produced in the republic and imported within the framework of projects, according to lists approved by the Cabinet of Ministers of the Republic of Uzbekistan;

[72] These privileges are available depending on the volume of foreign direct investments:

- from USD 300 000 to USD3m – for a period of three years;
- from USD3m to USD5m – for a period of five years;
- from USD5m to USD10m – for a period of seven years;
- from USD10m and above – for a period of ten years, with application of the profit tax rate and the single tax payment in the amount of 50% below the current rates for the next five years.

[73] For this purpose, investments made by legal entities and natural persons made without a guarantee from Uzbekistan are considered as foreign investments.

6.4.2 SIZ 'Angren' (Presidential Decree No. UP-4436)[33]

[74] Residents of SIZ 'Angren' are exempt from the payment of:

- income tax, property tax for legal entities, the tax on improvement and development of social infrastructure, the unified tax for small businesses, as well as mandatory contributions to the Republican Road Fund;
- customs duties (except customs charges) on equipment, components, and materials not produced in the country, which are imported into the territory of SIZ 'Angren' for the implementation of projects on the lists approved by the Cabinet of Ministers.

[75] The above exemptions are granted for a period of three to seven years depending on the number of investments made including the equivalent of:

- from USD300 000 to USD3m – for a period of three years;
- more than USD3m to USD10m – for a period of five years;
- more than USD10m – for a period of seven years.

6.4.3 SIZ 'Djizak' (Presidential Decree No. UP-4516)[34]

[76] Residents of SIZ 'Djizak' are exempt from the payment of:

- profit tax, corporate property tax, tax on improvement and development of social infrastructure, the unified tax for small businesses, as well as mandatory contributions to the Republican Road Fund;

---

[33] Presidential Decree 'On the Creation of a Free Economic Zone "Angren"' No. UP-4436 dated 13 Apr. 2012.
[34] Presidential Decree 'On the Creation of a Free Economic Zone "Dzhizak"' No. UP-4516 dated 18 Mar. 2013.

– customs payments (except for customs duties) for equipment, components, and materials not produced in the republic, which are imported to the territory of the SIZ 'Djizak' as part of the implementation of projects, according to the lists approved by the Cabinet of Ministers.

[77] The above benefits are granted for a period of three to seven years, depending on the amount of investment made, including the equivalent of:

– from USD300 000 to USD3m – for a period of three years;
– from USD3m to USD10m – for a period of five years;
– over USD10m – for a period of seven years.

[78] Foreign investment and other assets of foreign investors in Uzbekistan are not subject to nationalisation or requisition,[35] except for cases of natural disasters, accidents, epidemics, and epizootics (this being a disease event in a non-human animal population, analogous to an epidemic in humans).

[79] Under Article 10 of the Law on Foreign Investments and Investment activities, a foreign investor can independently and freely dispose of income derived from its investment (including its unimpeded repatriation), after payment of taxes and other mandatory payments. In this regard, the government guarantees investors both the freedom to choose the object and means of their investment, as well as the freedom to dispose of income from their investment activities.

[80] Accordingly, dividends and profits as well as proceeds from sales and interest on loans and fees and charges for IP or technology transfer are freely transferable abroad in accordance with the procedures specified in legislation.

[81] Financing is available from local and international banks and international financial institutions.

[82] Under local legislation,[36] security can be granted over the following assets:

– immovable property:
  (i) mortgage of a building or construction (or of a part of a building or construction), including the plot of land on which the building or construction is located;
  (ii) mortgage of an enterprise (as a property complex[37]);
– movable property:
  (i) pledge of movable property (i.e. equipment, machinery, motor vehicles, etc.);
  (ii) pledge of goods in the course of turnover (i.e. raw materials, goods in stock, semi-finished and finished products, etc.);

---

[35] Law of the Republic of Uzbekistan No. ZRU-598 'On investments and investment activities' dated 25 Dec. 2019, Art. 21.
[36] Law of the Republic of Uzbekistan No. 736-XII 'On pledge' No. 736-XII dated 9 Dec. 1992, Art. 5.
[37] Enterprise as a property complex includes all types of property designated for its activity, including land plots, buildings, constructions, equipment, inventory, raw materials, products, claims, debts and also rights to symbols identifying the enterprise, its products, works and services (i.e. company name, trademarks and service marks), and other exclusive rights, unless otherwise envisaged by law or contract (Art. 85 of the Civil Code).

  – property rights:
  (i) pledge of shares in a joint stock company;
  (ii) pledge of a participating interest in an LLC;
  (iii) pledge of a right of possession and use, including the right to lease, and other property rights.

[83] For a local/domestic company to open a bank account abroad is subject to a permit from the Central Bank.

7 SPECIFIC ISSUES OF COMPANY/SECURITIES LAW

7.1 Shareholder Approval

[84] Shareholder approval is generally required for major transactions, for transactions with affiliated parties and for any M&A transactions. The board of directors (the 'Board') of any merging company must pass a resolution to convene the company's general meeting of shareholders for the purpose of approving a Merger or a Merger Agreement. The Board of the non-surviving entity must also approve a deed of assignment (the 'Deed of Assignment') with respect to the Merger (this Deed specifies the assets and liabilities that are to be transferred and/or assumed as a result of the Merger) and arrange for this to be approved by the company's general meeting of shareholders. The general meeting of shareholders of each merging entity must then pass a resolution for approval of the Merger and the Merger Agreement. The general meeting of shareholders of the non-surviving company must then approve the Deed of Assignment. Participants have a pre-emptive right[38] to purchase shares offered for sale to a third party.

[85] Under the LLC law, if a participant is willing to sell his/her interest to another shareholder in the company, there is no need for the consent or approval of the company or other participants, unless otherwise envisaged by the charter of the LLC. If the participant intends to sell his/her shares (or part of a share) to a third party, he/she is required to notify the other members of the company about this in writing, as well as the company itself, specifying the price and other conditions for its sale.

[86] The LLC's charter may provide a pre-emptive right to purchase a share (or part of a share) disproportionately to the number of shares of the shareholders at its establishment based on a unanimous decision of the general meeting of the shareholders.[39]

[87] Under JSC law, if the number of shareholders does not exceed fifty, the company's charter may provide for pre-emptive rights. A shareholder selling his/her

---

[38] Law of the Republic of Uzbekistan No. 310-II 'On Company with Limited and Additional Responsibility' dated 6 Dec. 2001, Art. 20.
[39] *Ibid.*

shares to a third party is obliged to notify in writing, directly or through the company, the other shareholders of the intention to sell his/her shares, with an indication of the price and terms of the offer.[40]

7.2 Directors' Duties

[88] In accordance with the LLC and JSC Laws, an LLC and JSC are entitled to have a Directorate (or a Board) as a collective executive organ. The charter of the company determines the powers/ competence of the Directorate. The charter and a regulation relating to the Directorate (if any) determines the operating procedures and methods of adopting resolutions by the Directorate.

[89] The members of the Directorate must act in good faith in their capacity as members of the Directorate, in a reasonable manner and always in the interests of the company. The law fails to be specific as to the meaning of 'good faith, a reasonable manner and in the interests of the company'. Negligent performance of duty, inaction and abuse of office may be regarded as examples of NOT acting in good faith, or in a reasonable manner or in the interests of the company.

[90] Since the Directorate is a collective organ, the liability of its members is joint and several.[41] Meanwhile, an individual claim seeking the satisfaction of losses caused by actions (or omissions) of a member of the Directorate may be brought against that member of the Directorate (rather than against ALL members of the Directorate); the LLC or any of its participants are entitled to bring such a claim before the court.[42]

7.3 Form of Consideration

[91] Under the JSC and LLC laws, shares can be issued both for cash and non-cash consideration. The Civil Code[43] specifies that a non-cash consideration can be paid in the form of assets, property rights, property use rights and other property (i.e. the provision of works and services). The monetary value of non-cash contributions must be agreed between the founders of the company. There are no restrictions on the subsequent disposal of shares acquired as the result of a contribution-in-kind.

---

[40] Law of the Republic of Uzbekistan N223-I 'On Joint-Stock Companies and Protection of the Shareholders' Rights' dated 26 Apr. 1996, Art. 6.

[41] *Ibid*. (n 40 LLC), Art. 42, para. 4.

[42] *Ibid*., para. 5.

[43] Article 58 – in the company (in JSC and LLC) contributions can be money, securities, other things or property rights or other alienable rights having a monetary value.

7.4 Financial Assistance

[92] Uzbek legislation does not restrict members of the target group from issuing a guarantee as security for loans granted to an acquiring company.

[93] There is no clear concept of 'financial assistance' in Uzbek law. In practice, funds can be provided in the form of a 'shareholder loan' from the founders of the company to the company.

7.5 Security Interests

[94] Under Uzbek legislation, loans can be secured by a pledge of movable assets, rights, or by pledges of immovable property (mortgages).

[95] The concepts of 'floating charge' and 'fixed charge' do not exist in Uzbek legislation. The most common forms of security are the pledge and suretyship (if issued by companies) or guarantees (if issued by banks). The registration of these securities depends on the type of collateral:
- a pledge of immovable property is subject to state registration with the state 'cadastre' (this being the official record of the owners of land and of the amount and value of the land they own, used for calculating the amount of tax owed);
- a pledge of shares is subject to registration with the state body regulating the securities market;
- a pledge of movable assets (e.g. shares, bonds) is subject to mandatory state registration, as it requires the consent of the state authority;
- a pledge of assets, e.g. (i) a pledge of movable property (i.e. equipment, machinery, or motor vehicles, etc.) or (ii) a pledge of goods in the course of turnover (i.e. raw materials, goods in stock, semi-finished and finished products, etc.), is subject to registration with state authorities.

[96] There are no specific registration requirements (in terms of their validity) applicable to guarantees.

7.6 Purchase of Own Shares

[97] Subject to a decision of the General Meeting of Shareholders on the reduction of the company's Charter Capital, a company has the right to acquire some of the shares issued/ placed by it and to reduce their total number. This also involves a decision of the Supervisory Board of the company for the purpose of their subsequent resale in accordance with established procedures.

[98] Every shareholder who is an owner of shares of a certain type, the acquisition of which was based on a signed decision, is entitled to sell some or all of such shares, and the company is obliged to acquire them, in circumstances where share-holders voted against or did not participate in the voting for valid reasons when the General Shareholder's Meeting made decisions on:

- the reorganisation of the company; or
- the consolidation of outstanding shares; or
- a major transaction related to the acquisition or disposal of property by the company; or
- where amendments and additions were made to the company's charter or a new edition of the company's charter was approved, which restricted share-holders' rights.

[99] If the total quantity of applications received from a company's shareholders for the acquisition by the company of their shares exceeds the number of shares that can be acquired by the company in accordance with the limitations established by the relevant provisions of JSC law, the shares available for purchase must be acquired from the shareholders in proportion to their declared demands.

[100] The acquisition by a company of its own shares must be carried out independently or through professional participants in the securities market unless otherwise established by law.[44]

7.7 The Corporate Veil

[101] In accordance with the JSC law, a company may have a subsidiary and associated companies in the forms of a JSC or an LLC. A subsidiary is not liable for the obligations of its parent company. The parent company, which is entitled to give to its subsidiary's obligatory instructions, bears joint responsibility with its subsidiaries for transactions concluded by the latter in pursuance of any such mandatory instructions.

[102] In the case of bankruptcy of a subsidiary company which is caused through the parent company's fault, the latter bears responsibility for the subsidiary's obligations. The bankruptcy of a subsidiary is considered to be caused by the fault of the parent company only in cases when the parent company has given the subsidiary a mandatory instruction and (or) has used the opportunity to commit the subsidiary to a specific action, knowing full well that the bankruptcy of the subsidiary will occur as a result.

7.8 Insolvency

[103] Where external management is involved as part of bankruptcy proceedings the external management plan may provide for the following measures to restore a debtor's financial solvency:

---

[44] *Ibid.* (n 42) Art. 37.

- conversion of production to cash;
- closure of unprofitable businesses;
- recovery of accounts receivable;
- sale of a part of the debtor's property;
- assignment of the debtor's claims;
- performance of the debtor's obligations by third parties;
- the issue of additional shares of the debtor;
- sale of the enterprise (business) of the debtor as a property complex;
- substitution of the debtor's assets.

[104] Article 110 of the Law on Bankruptcy[45] governs the procedure for the sale of an enterprise (business) of a debtor as a 'property complex' (meaning the undertaking and assets). The regulation 'On the Procedure for the Evaluation and Realisation of Enterprises under Restructuring and Bankruptcy Processes'[46] also stipulates the procedure for evaluating and determining the initial sale price in the open tender process where the property of an enterprise is being sold, against which a bankruptcy process has been applied by a court ruling.

[105] Selling an enterprise (business) as a property complex can be planned for in the external management plan as a measure for the financial recovery of the debtor and correspondingly for settlements with creditors. The sale of the enterprise (business) is carried out through an open tender, which is conducted through competitive tendering or auction, in the manner stipulated by Article 380 of the Civil Code. The form and conditions for holding a tender are determined by the creditors' meeting (creditors' committee). The enterprise (business) is put up for auction at a price decided by a resolution of the creditors' meeting. The initial sale price is based on the value of the enterprise (or its business) as evaluated by an appraiser and can be above or below the evaluated value.

[106] The external manager must publish an announcement concerning the sale of the enterprise (business) by open tender in an official gazette at least thirty days prior to the tender. If no one, or only one applicant, applies within the period referred to in the announcement, the tender for the sale of the enterprise (business) is deemed to have failed. In this case, a new tender is held under the same conditions as the first tender. The sale price at the new tender may be reduced by 10% according to the resolution of the creditors' meeting or creditors' committee.

7.9 Choice of Law

[107] Uzbek law recognises choice of law principles for contractual obligations. However, the choice of foreign law will not exclude the application of mandatory

---

[45] No. 474-II dated 24 Apr. 2003.
[46] Annex No. 1 to the Resolution of the Cabinet of Ministers of the Republic of Uzbekistan on measures to improve the efficiency of the restructuring and financial recovery of economically insolvent enterprises No. 188 dated 18 Apr. 2003.

rules of Uzbek law, which cannot be derogated from by agreement between the parties. According to Uzbek law, regardless of the choice of law applicable to the relations of the parties, certain mandatory rules of Uzbek law must still be applied.[47]

[108] The Republic of Uzbekistan is a party to the United Nations Convention on the Recognition and Enforcement of Foreign Arbitral Awards 1958 (the 'New York Convention') and, accordingly, an arbitral award should generally be recognised and enforceable in Uzbekistan under the New York Convention provided the conditions for enforcement set out in the New York Convention are met.

[109] We note, however, that in practice reliance upon international treaties can require the relevant Uzbekistan officials (including courts) to be supplied with more information as to the effect of and procedures under the treaty, which may not be entirely consistent with Uzbek legislation relating to procedure or with Uzbek court rules. This could delay enforcement procedures in the Republic of Uzbekistan. Further, the result of a request for the recognition and enforcement of a foreign arbitral award rendered in connection with an arbitration proceeding occurring outside of the Republic of Uzbekistan may prove to be difficult to predict because the court system of the Republic of Uzbekistan is not always independent from interference.

[110] However, an Uzbek court may refuse the recognition and enforcement of foreign arbitral awards in full or in part if one of the following grounds exists:

- a party to the arbitration agreement was in any way incapable of entering into the agreement by the law applicable to it, or the arbitration agreement was invalid under the chosen governing law, (or, in the absence of any chosen governing law – under the law of the country where the foreign arbitral award has been rendered);
- a party against which a foreign arbitral award has been rendered has not been timely and duly notified about the proceedings, their time and place, or due to other reasons could not provide its explanations;
- a foreign arbitral award has been rendered in a dispute not provided for or not subject to the terms of the arbitration agreement or arbitration clause in the contract, or contains rulings on matters beyond the scope of the arbitration agreement or arbitration clause in the contract, unless the rulings on those matters covered by the arbitration agreement can properly be separated from those not covered by such agreement;
- a composition of the arbitration body or the arbitration process did not comply with the agreement of the parties or, in the absence of such agreement, did not comply with the law of the country where the arbitration took place;
- a foreign arbitral award was not final for the parties or was cancelled, or suspended by the competent authority of the state where it was rendered, or of the country whose laws were being applied;
- a dispute was resolved by an incompetent foreign court or arbitration body.[48]

---

[47] Article 1158 of the Civil Code.
[48] Economic Procedure Code of the Republic of Uzbekistan dated 24 Jan. 2018, Art. 255.

[111] The court may also refuse to recognise and enforce a foreign arbitral award if:

- enforcement of a foreign arbitral award would contradict the 'public order' of the Republic of Uzbekistan;
- the subject matter of the dispute may not be subject to arbitration under the laws of the Republic of Uzbekistan;
- the statute of limitations for the enforcement of a foreign arbitral award has expired.[49]

8 SPECIFIC RULES ON PUBLIC TAKEOVERS

[112] There are no specific rules or normative acts in Uzbekistan addressing public takeovers.

[113] However, there are laws on joint stock companies, the protection of shareholders' rights, and the law on LLCs, which regulate relations regarding the creation, reorganisation, and liquidation of JSCs and limited and additional liability companies, as well as the protection of shareholders' rights.

[114] Chapter 4 of the Law on Limited and Additional Liability Companies[50] and Chapter 10 of the Law on JSCs[51] include information on the reorganisation of a company. These two laws are considered the main laws governing the reorganisation of companies.

9 OTHER RELEVANT LAWS AND DUE DILIGENCE ISSUES

9.1 Anti-corruption

[115] The main laws regulating anti-corruption issues are:

- The Code on Administrative Responsibility adopted by Law No. 2015-XII dated 22 September 1994, as amended ('Administrative Code');
- The Criminal Code adopted by Law No. 2012-XII dated 22 September 1994, as amended ('Criminal Code');
- The Law 'On Transparency of the Activities of State Power and Management Bodies' No. ZRU-369 dated 5 May 2014, as amended;
- The Law 'On Combating Corruption' No. ZRU-419 dated 3 January 2017 ('Anti-corruption Law');
- The Law 'On State Purchases' No. ZRU-684 dated 22 April 2021;
- The Law 'On Public Control' No. ZRU-474 dated 12 April 2018;

---

[49] *Ibid.*
[50] Law on Limited and Additional Liability Companies No. 310-II dated 6 Dec. 2001
[51] Law on Joint Stock Companies No. ZRU-531 dated 20 Mar. 2019.

- The Law 'On Measures for Further Improvement of the Anti-corruption System in the Republic of Uzbekistan' No. UP-5729 dated 27 May 2019;
- The State Programme 'On Combating Corruption for 2021–2022', Appendix No. 1 to the Resolution of the President No. UP-6257 dated 6 July 2021, as amended;
- Order of the Ministry of Justice of the Republic of Uzbekistan No. 3287 'On Approval of the Regulations on the Procedure of Anti-corruption Examination of the Normative Legal Acts and their Projects' dated 24 February 2021.

[116] The Anti-corruption Law is vaguely written and specifies:

- basic principles for fighting corruption;
- the government authorities in charge of combating/preventing corruption;
- measures for increasing public awareness on the prevention of corruption;
- measures on preventing corruption, etc.

[117] The Anti-corruption Law established the Interdepartmental Commission for Combating Corruption[52] (the '**Commission**') in order to coordinate the activities of bodies and organisations that carry out and participate in anti-corruption activities.

[118] Any decisions taken by the Commission are binding on all government bodies and public administrations, public associations and other organisations.[53]

[119] The Commission carries out its activities in cooperation with state bodies, other organisations, as well as territorial interdepartmental commissions on combating corruption. The president approves the members of the Commission and controls its activity.

[120] Over the last two years, the government has increased its focus on fighting corruption and a number of reforms are ongoing in the government sector in order to make various processes transparent and to eliminate corruption in the country.

9.2 Environmental Law

[121] The law on environmental expertise[54] provides for the compliance of planned or ongoing economic and other activities with environmental requirements and determines the admissibility of their implementation in conformity with environmental expertise. Environmental inspection is carried out in order to determine:

- compliance with environmental requirements for the projected economic and other activities, at the stages preceding the decision on their implementation;

---

[52] Law of the Republic of Uzbekistan No. ZRU-419 'On Anti-corruption' dated 3 Jan. 2017, Art. 2.
[53] *Ibid.*
[54] No. 73-II dated 25 May 2000.

- the level of environmental hazard of the planned or ongoing economic and other activities that may negatively impact the state of the environment and the health of citizens;
- the sufficiency and validity of the measures provided for environmental protection and the rational use of natural resources.

[122] The matters requiring state ecological expertise are:

- projects and proposals for state programs, concepts, placement schemes and the development of productive facilities, branches of economy and the social sphere;
- materials of choice for all types of construction on real estate;
- pre-project and project documentation;
- draft technical and instruction documents regulating economic and other activities related to the use of natural resources;
- documentation on the creation of new types of equipment, technologies, materials, substances and products;
- existing enterprises and other facilities that have a negative impact on the environment and the health of citizens;
- materials involved in complex surveys of specific territories for the purpose of assigning them the status of protected natural territories, or zones of potential ecological emergency or ecological disaster;
- all types of urban planning documentation;
- matters subject to a special legal regime.

9.3 Product Safety

[123] In accordance with the law on the quality and safety of food products,[55] state regulation in the field of quality and safety of food products is carried out by establishing veterinary and sanitary rules and norms, phytosanitary standards (meaning standards for the control of plant diseases especially in agricultural crops), rules and hygienic standards, state standards, technical conditions containing requirements for the quality and safety of food products, and the conditions of production, procurement, processing, supply, storage, transportation and sale of food products.

[124] Rules and regulations on the quality and safety of food products are approved by state bodies in the manner prescribed by law and are mandatory for legal entities and individuals operating in the field of food products.

[125] Food products, as well as equipment intended for the manufacture of food products or for use in contact with food products, can be produced and imported into the territory of Uzbekistan, and can be sold and used after assessing their compliance with the requirements of standards and regulations on the quality and safety of food products and their state registration.

---

[55] No. 483-I dated 30 Aug. 1997.

[126] The list of products subjects to mandatory certification and the procedures for certification are specified in Annex No. 1 to the resolution of the Cabinet of Ministers, as also the list of products produced in Uzbekistan and imported into its territory subject to mandatory certification, No. 122 dated 28 28 April 2011.

9.4 Intellectual Property

[127] The Law 'On Copyright and Related Rights'[56] regulates the relations arising in connection with the creation and use of works of science, literature, and art (copyright), performances, phonograms (meaning symbols representing a vocal sound), broadcasts or cable broadcasting organisations. The copyright for a work of science, literature, and art arises from the fact of its creation. The creation and exercise of a copyright do not require registration of the work or any other formalities. A person designated as the author on the original or a copy of the work is considered to be its author unless proven otherwise.

[128] In Uzbekistan, relations arising in connection with trademarks are regulated by the Law 'On Trademarks, Service Marks and Appellations of Origin of goods'.[57] Legal protection of a trademark (service mark) arises as a result of its registration. The trademark can be registered in any colour or colour combinations.

[129] A certificate of trademark registration is issued after the examination of the claimed designation and is valid for ten years with the possibility of an extension every ten years.

[130] It is necessary to apply to the state patent office of Uzbekistan to register a trademark.

9.5 Valuation of Intellectual Property

[131] The national standard of property valuation of Uzbekistan (NSPV No. 13) 'valuation of intellectual property' defines the rules and regulations for the valuation of intellectual property and intangible assets, establishes definitions, information requirements, the procedure for evaluation, approaches, methods of evaluation, and requirements for registration of valuation results.

[132] Items which may be the subject of valuation under NSPV No. 13 are as follows:

- works of science, literature, and art;
- performances, phonograms, broadcasting or cable broadcastings;
- inventions, industrial designs, utility models;
- programs for electronic computers and databases;

---

[56] Law on Copyright and Related Rights No. ZRU-42 dated 20 Jul. 2006.
[57] Law 'On Trademarks, Service Marks and Appellations of Origin of Goods' No. 267-II dated 30 Aug. 2001.

- designs of integrated circuits;
- new varieties of plants;
- undisclosed information, including production secrets (know-how, including geological and other commercial information about the natural environment);
- company names as part of a comprehensive business licence;
- trademarks, service marks, and appellations of origin of goods.

[133] The cost (value) of these subjects for assessment is determined considering the property rights relating to them, including any associated difficulties and/or restrictions related to such rights.

[134] The valuation of intangible assets and intellectual property consists of the following steps:

- determination of the relevant evaluation task and conclusion of a contract for valuation of the relevant object;
- identification of the object to be valued;
- information collection and analysis;
- selection, justification, and application of relevant assessment approaches and methods;
- coordination of the results obtained by the application of different approaches towards evaluation and determination of the final cost of the valuation;
- preparation of the valuation report.

10 THE DUE DILIGENCE PROCESS

[135] Sellers will likely be familiar with the concept of a full due diligence exercise if they have received prior financing from the European Bank for Reconstruction and Development (EBRD), or from the Islamic Corporation for the Development of the Private Sector (ICD) or from other international financial institutions. Noting that the economy was closed until recently, not many M&A transactions took place in Uzbekistan. While property issues are usually investigated as part of due diligence, reliance is usually placed only on a review of documents provided by the seller rather than on an independent search of the records.

[136] Both virtual and physical data rooms are used, but not very often. Mainly companies having majority foreign ownership use a 'data room'. For a local company, it will be unusual to maintain a 'data room'.

[137] The critical issues to be addressed when conducting due diligence in Uzbekistan depend on the specific sector in which the target company operates. For transactions in the mining and petroleum sectors, particular emphasis will be placed on investigating whether the subsurface user has met the obligations under its agreed work programme for carrying out exploration and/or production. In addition, it is critical to investigate prior transfers of ownership of the relevant assets to confirm

that all necessary consents were given. In each case, failure to have fulfilled obligations or to have obtained consents can lead to termination of the subsurface use rights (i.e. the rights in the relevant exploration or production contract).

[138] The imposition of contractual representations, warranties and indemnities is common. While such concepts are not explicitly provided for by Uzbek law, these are often used in transaction documents (especially in high-value deals) drafted under foreign law to address particular issues found during due diligence. Because Uzbek law does not explicitly recognise representations, warranties and indemnities, the enforceability of such provisions by Uzbek courts is not certain.

11 ROLES OF THE COURTS

[139] The parties to an agreement may agree to submit disputes arising out of the agreement to the courts or to arbitration[58] in a jurisdiction other than Uzbekistan, except for cases when Uzbek law requires otherwise (e.g. cases relating to rights to immovable property located in Uzbekistan).[59]

[140] The Uzbek judicial system is not fully independent and also may be subject to outside influence. Courts, and especially regional courts, are sometimes reluctant to issue rulings against local state authorities.

[141] Judgments by Uzbek courts and awards by local arbitration courts are enforceable. Decisions by local arbitration courts may be appealed to the local courts based on specific grounds stipulated in the Economic Procedural Code (these grounds being mostly related to procedural violations).

[142] Under Uzbek law, foreign court judgments can be enforced in Uzbekistan (i) if such enforcement is expressly stipulated by law, (ii) if there is an applicable treaty between Uzbekistan and such foreign jurisdiction that provides for reciprocal enforcement of court judgments or (iii) based on the principle of reciprocity. Uzbek legislation does not include clear rules on the application of the principle of reciprocity. Thus, there can be no assurance that the courts of Uzbekistan will recognise and enforce a judgment rendered by courts of a jurisdiction with which Uzbekistan has no agreement based on the principle of reciprocity.

[143] Uzbekistan is not a party to multilateral or bilateral treaties with many countries for the mutual enforcement of court judgments, except for a limited number of treaties which are primarily with Commonwealth of Independent States (CIS) countries – these being the countries which were formed when the former Soviet Union (now called Russia) totally dissolved in 1991.

[144] Uzbekistan is a signatory to the New York Convention. Therefore, an arbitral award that is rendered in a New York Convention participating state (including the

---

58 Law 'On international commercial arbitration' No. ZRU-674 dated 16 Feb. 2021, adopted by the Legislative Chamber on 5 Aug. 2020, approved by the Senate on 11 Sep. 2020, but the act has not yet entered into force.
59 Civil Code of the Republic of Uzbekistan dated 29 Aug. 1996

United Kingdom and the United States of America) should generally be recognised and enforced in Uzbekistan provided that the conditions for enforcement set out in the New York Convention are met and the award is filed with the relevant Uzbek court for recognition and enforcement in accordance with the Economic Procedural Code, which provides statutory guidelines for the enforcement of arbitral awards.

[145] The principle of reciprocity, on reasonable interpretation, means that a court Judgment and arbitral award rendered in a foreign country will be enforced in Uzbekistan, provided that a court Judgment and arbitral award rendered in Uzbekistan would be enforced in the relevant foreign country. It is assumed that court judgments and arbitral awards rendered in Uzbekistan would be enforced in a foreign country unless otherwise proven.

[146] Foreign companies have successfully obtained judgments and awards against Uzbek state authorities and local Uzbek companies before domestic courts. For example, foreign companies have been successful in disputes involving taxes, payment of duties, claims against imposed fines and contractual disputes.

[147] As a general rule confidentiality provisions safeguarding confidential information and trade secrets are usually enforceable in Uzbekistan.

[148] In reality, there are very few protections available to minority investors.

[149] Uzbek law has no concept of warranties and indemnities. Therefore, it is unlikely that warranties and indemnities as known in the United Kingdom or similar jurisdictions will be enforced in Uzbekistan if they are provided for in an agreement governed by Uzbek law.

[150] Courts in Uzbekistan are relatively efficient and claims in courts can be pursued relatively quickly based on the statutory time limits for consideration of claims in courts. It is not generally an expensive process, although most claims require payment of a state duty of up to 3% of the value of the claim.

[151] The following courts are established In Uzbekistan:

- Constitutional Court of Uzbekistan;
- Supreme Court of Uzbekistan;
- Military Court;
- Civil Court of the Republic of Karakalpakstan, regional and Tashkent city Civil Courts;
- Criminal Court of the Republic of Karakalpakstan, regional and Tashkent city Criminal Courts;
- Economic Courts of the Republic of Karakalpakstan, regions and the city of Tashkent;
- Administrative Courts of the Republic of Karakalpakstan, regions and the city of Tashkent;
- Inter-district, District (city) Civil Courts;
- District (city) Criminal Courts;
- Inter-district, District (city) Economic Courts;
- District (city) Administrative Courts.

[152] Any civil, economic or criminal case, as well as cases involving an administrative offence, can go through several stages of consideration in the courts.

[153] The first stage consideration of the case on its merits is at the Court of First Instance. The Court of First Instance is not necessarily a judicial institution at the lowest level; rather, 'first instance' means that the case is being considered for the first time in a court. Thus, even the Supreme Court of Uzbekistan can act as a Court of First Instance. It all depends on the importance of the case.[60]

[154] The second stage is the review of the decision (sentence) of the court by a higher court on appeal or 'cassation' on the complaint of any party or on protest of the Prosecutor. (A court of 'cassation' is a higher-instance appellate court that does not re-examine the facts of a case, but only interprets the relevant law, differing in this respect from those systems which have a supreme court able to rule on both the facts of a case and the relevant law. The term derives from the Latin *cassare*, 'to reverse/overturn').

[155] Here it is necessary to understand that the decision of the Court of First Instance comes into force not at once, but rather only after a certain time. For decisions of courts in civil cases the time period is twenty days; in criminal cases and in cases of administrative offences – ten days; in economic cases – one month. Thus, the type of proceedings under review affects whether the court decision has entered into force or not.

[156] Thus, the appeal procedure is a review of the decisions (sentences) of the court that have not yet entered into force through the re-conduct of a full trial. Cassation proceedings are a review, by partial judicial proceedings, of decisions (sentences) of the court that have already entered into force.

[157] The third stage is the review of decisions 'in the order of supervision'. In criminal proceedings and proceedings on administrative offences, supervisory proceedings may be initiated only after the case has been heard on appeal or cassation. In civil and economic proceedings, this does not matter, but most often, the review in the supervisory procedure takes place after the case has been heard in the court of second instance. Thus, it can be called a kind of third round. Its most important feature is that the parties no longer have the right to initiate a new review of the case themselves. Only authorised officials of the courts and the Prosecutor's office, who can file protests in this respect, have the right to do so. The parties can only file a complaint to these authorised persons, being the persons who will decide whether to make a protest (i.e. further appeal) or not.

[158] Court costs consist of the state fee and costs associated with the consideration of the case. The amount of the costs is determined by the type of claim:

- in claims for the recovery of money – by the amount of money being sought;
- in claims for reclamation of property – the value of the property claimed;

---

[60] Civil Procedure Code of the Republic of Uzbekistan dated, ch 14; Criminal Procedure Code of the Republic of Uzbekistan dated 22 Oct. 1994, Ch. 48; Economic Procedure Code of the Republic of Uzbekistan dated 24 Jan. 2018, Ch. 3; Code on Administrative Responsibilities of the Republic of Uzbekistan dated 22 Sep. 1994, Chs 18, 22.

- for several claims – the total amount of all claims;
- in claims for urgent payments and urgent issues – the sum of all payments or issues, but for no more than three years;
- in claims without term, or for lifelong payments and disbursements – the sum of payments or disbursements for three years;
- in claims for the reduction or increase of payments or disbursements – the amount by which payments or disbursements are reduced or increased, but for not more than one year;
- in claims for the termination of payments or disbursements — the sum of the remaining payments or disbursements, but for not more than one year;
- in claims for early termination of a property lease agreement, the sum of payments for the use of the property during the remaining term of the agreement, but for not more than three years;
- in claims relating to property rights to constructions belonging to citizens on private property – the market value of the construction, but not below the 'cadastral' value or, in the absence of a cadastral value, not below the assessment of the construction for compulsory insurance purposes, and for buildings owned by organisations – not below the actual assessment value of the construction.[61]

12 MERGER CONTROLS: ANTITRUST/ COMPETITION ISSUES

12.1 Relevant Legislation and Competent Authorities

[159] The Law on Competition[62] is the primary legislation regulating relations in the field of competition in the commodity and financial markets. Based on this law, the Antimonopoly authority is the responsible organ for merger control. The Antimonopoly authority issues a preliminary consent to the acquisition or merger of certain entities, as described below.

[160] According to the Law on Competition, the Antimonopoly authority and its territorial authorities are responsible for merger controls.

[161] The Antimonopoly authority implements state policy in the field of competition in the commodity and financial markets aimed at limiting and suppressing anti-competitive actions and unfair competition, and preventing illegal actions of public administrative bodies and public authorities.

[162] Preliminary consent of the Antimonopoly authority to M&A transactions is necessary in cases where the total book value of assets of the seller, or the seller's total revenue from the sale of goods for the last calendar year, exceeds 100,000

---

[61] Civil Procedure Code, Art. 129.
[62] No. ZRU-319 dated 6 Jan. 2012.

times the monthly minimum wage (BCR), or where one of them is an entity occupying a dominant position in the relevant commodity or financial market.

[163] The requirements referred to above do not apply to mergers and acquisitions of legal entities where this is determined by decision of the President or of the Cabinet of Ministers.

[164] The procedure for issuing a preliminary consent to a relevant merger or acquisition is determined by the Cabinet of Ministers.

12.2 Scope of the Controls

[165] The Antimonopoly authority issues a preliminary consent to the merger or acquisition, the requirements for which are referred to above. In addition, prior consent may be required for certain transactions for the acquisition of shares in the share capital of an entity by a person or group of persons.

[166] In such a situation, the preliminary consent of the Antimonopoly authority is necessary if:

- such person or group of persons is entitled to control more than 50% of listed shares;
- the total balance-sheet value of assets or the total revenue from the sale of goods for the last calendar year of the parties to the transaction exceeds 100,000 times the BCR, or one of the parties to the transaction is an entity that holds a dominant position in the commodity or financial market.

12.3 Process/Mechanics

[167] In some cases, the consent of the Antimonopoly authority is not required. Nevertheless, in the case of a merger, accession, or acquisition of shares in the share capital (as defined above), a person or a group of persons must submit to the centres of public services the following documents prior to the transaction:

- the application for prior consent to carry out the relevant transaction;
- the passport data of the applicant – (for an individual the series and number of the passport, the date, and place of issue, and the issuing authority);
- information on the types of activity involved, the types of goods and their volumes produced and sold by the applicant within the two years preceding the date of application (or during the period of activity, if this is less than two years);
- the financial and statistical reporting for the previous two calendar years;
- information on the composition of the group of persons, indicating the reasons why such persons are included in this group, and other information relating to the relevant transactions for the acquisition of shares.

[168] The Antimonopoly authority has the right to give prior consent to M&A transactions and/or to make such consent dependent on particular requirements for ensuring competition rules.

[169] At the same time, any such requirements, as well as the terms of their fulfilment, should be contained in the decision of the Antimonopoly authority on the preliminary consent to the merger or accession, or on the preliminary consent to relevant transactions for the acquisition of shares in the share capital. If the performance of these actions or transactions may lead to the emergence or strengthening of a dominant position of the relevant entity or group of persons in the relevant commodity or financial market and (or) to a restriction on competition, those entities and (or) individuals who have committed to carrying out these actions or transactions must, at the request of the Antimonopoly authority, take measures to restore the necessary conditions of competition.

[170] According to the results of their review, the Special Commission should, no later than ten calendar days from the date of receipt of the necessary documents and information, decide to issue (or refuse to issue) a preliminary consent to the creation of the association or merger, or to the acquisition of the relevant entity.[63]

[171] In cases where the Antimonopoly authority has reasonable grounds to assume that the action in question will lead, or may lead, to a restriction of competition,[64] the application review period may be extended, but not by more than one month, if so requested by the applicant. In practice, it may take up to one month to obtain consent due to the time required to provide the authority with all the requested documents. The decision to issue or refuse to issue a preliminary consent to the creation of an association or merger, or to the acquisition of an entity, must be signed in duplicate by the Chairman and members of the Special Commission and must be certified by the stamp of the Antimonopoly authority. The decision made by the Special Commission, notifying the result of their consideration of the application, must be sent to the authorised representative no later than one working day after the date of its adoption.

[172] Interested parties involved in actions to create an association or merger, or the acquisition of a legal entity may, on their written request, be provided with a copy of the relevant decision.

[173] There is no fee for issuing a decision.

[174] The Antimonopoly authority has the right to refuse to give preliminary permission to the applicant if:

- grant of the application for preliminary consent may lead to the emergence or strengthening of a dominant position of the relevant entity or group of

---

[63] Decree of the Cabinet of Ministers 'On Approval of some Administrative Regulations for Rendering Public Services in the Sphere of Antimonopoly Regulation in Commodity and Financial Markets' No. 338 dated 28 May 2020, Annex 2, Art. 19.

[64] Including in connection with the emergence or strengthening of the dominant position of enterprises or newly formed legal persons on the commodity or financial market.

persons in the relevant commodity or financial market and (or) to a restriction on competition;
- on considering the submitted documents, it was found that information contained in them was inaccurate or false.

[175] Violation of antimonopoly requirements for mergers, accessions, and transactions for the acquisition of shares and other property rights entail the imposition of a fine on citizens (from one to three times the BCR) and on executives (from five to ten times the BCR).

[176] Committing concerted actions or transactions that lead or may lead to a restriction of competition and/or to abuse of a dominant position in the commodity or financial markets, as well as violation of Antimonopoly requirements in respect of competitive tendering or exchange trading, entails the imposition of penalties on citizens (from three to five times the BCR) and on executives (from five to ten times the BCR[65]).

13 TAXATION ASPECTS

13.1 Nature of the Tax Regime

[177] Uzbek legislation regarding the scope of taxation is certain and clear and is detailed in the Tax Code, which is the primary legal source of tax law in the country. Uzbek tax law is based on the principles of compulsion, certainty, fairness, the unity of the taxation system, the openness of tax law, and the presumption of correctness on the part of the taxpayer.[66]

[178] Authorised bodies that enforce tax law are the State Tax Committee, the State Customs Committee, the Ministry of Finance, and state bodies and organisations that are responsible for levies of other due payments.[67] The Uzbek government has determined several strategies for further economic development, under which the tax system should be simplified and taxes decreased. It has accepted that the current tax system does not correspond to modern requirements, restrains the further development of the economy, does not stimulate expansion and modernisation of production, and does not create favourable conditions for doing business in Uzbekistan. Therefore, some crucial reforms in taxation have already taken place, while others are to be introduced in the coming years.

---

[65] Article 178 of the Administrative Responsibility Code as amended through 2001 (No. 2015-XII of 1994).
[66] Tax Code, Art. 5 (Principles of tax law).
[67] Tax Code, Art. 44 (Authorised bodies).

13.2 Liability to Tax

[179] Under Uzbek law, the income of residents or non-residents which is derived from the territory of Uzbekistan is subject to taxation. According to the Uzbek Tax Code, business vehicles are subject to the following taxes and other due payments:

- Corporate income tax
- Personal income tax
- Value-added tax
- Excise tax
- Taxes and special payments for subsoil users
- Tax for the use of water resources
- Property tax
- Land tax
- Tax on the consumption of gasoline, diesel fuel and gas for vehicles
- Unified social payment
- Insurance premiums of citizens to the extra-budgetary Pension Fund
- Mandatory contributions to state trust funds
- Mandatory contributions to individual accumulative pension accounts (INPS) of citizens
- Customs payments
- Fees for the right to retail trade of certain types of goods and the provision of certain types of services.

[180] Permanent establishments (PEs) are obliged to pay:

- Income tax (the sum of taxed income cannot be less than 7% of the expense rate[68])
- Tax on the use of water resources
- Property tax.

[181] As regards income tax of natural persons and other social taxes on employees (if they are receiving salaries or other income from a PE which is tax resident in Uzbekistan), the income tax payable is withheld from the employee's salary by the employer, which must pay it to the tax authorities. The employer is also liable to pay social taxes to the tax authorities (which amounts are not withheld from salaries). If a non-resident company has several PEs in Uzbekistan, it is liable to pay taxes for all its PEs (without any right of tax consolidation). Furthermore, value-added tax will be imposed on a company/resident in respect of services rendered by a PE within the territory of Uzbekistan.

[182] Corporate income tax (CIT) is paid by business vehicles on profits earned in Uzbekistan. This requirement refers to both residents, non-residents owning a PE

---

[68] Tax Code, Art. 154 – expenses of a legal entity that has a PE in Uzbekistan are all the expenses associated with the income gained in Uzbekistan through PE, disregarding whether these expenses were incurred in Uzbekistan or abroad.

in Uzbekistan, and non-resident profits not associated with the PE.[69] As of 1 January 2019, the corporate income tax was united with the tax on well-being and development of social infrastructure.[70] As a result, the corporate income tax rate is currently 14% (previously it was 7.5% for CIT, plus 8% for the tax on well-being and development of social infrastructure).

Value Added Tax (VAT)

[183] Substantial reforms are anticipated in the scope of VAT. The Uzbek government has launched its Conception for the Reform of the Tax System, which calls for a decrease in the rate of VAT from 20% to 12%. However, all business entities will be liable to pay VAT, as well as individual entrepreneurs, if they have a turnover of more than 1 bn Uzbekistan Soms (UZS) per year.[71]

Stamp Duties or Other Taxes on Land Transactions

[184] Under Uzbek law, stamp duties do not exist. In Uzbekistan, legal entities and individuals are subject to state duties as appropriate. Notaries charge legal persons state duties for land or real estate transactions. The rate of duty depends on the location of the real estate and its total area. For instance, rates for real estate in Tashkent, Nukus and other regional centres vary from 1–3 times the BCR, while in other localities the rates vary from 0.5–1.5 times the BCR.

Other Taxes on Land or Real Estate

[185] The Tax Code obliges commercial entities to pay tax on land in their ownership or possession, or which they use or rent.

Customs and Excise Duties

[186] For the transfer of goods and vehicles, commercial entities are required to pay:
- Customs fees
- VAT
- Excise tax
- Customs duty.

[187] Payers of excise tax are legal and natural persons that:
- produce goods taxable for excise tax in the territory of Uzbekistan;
- import excise goods into the customs territory of Uzbekistan;
- are a partner in charge of administration in a general partnership that produces excise goods.[72]

---

69 Tax Code, Art. 117-155.
70 Presidential Edict No. PP-3454 dated 29 Dec. 2017, addendum No. 7.
71 USD 1 = UZS 10542.66 (12 May 2021).
72 Tax Code, Chs VIII and XVIII.

13.3 Tax Consolidation

[188] Under the Tax Code, subsidiaries are liable to pay tax separately from their parent companies, if they have separate property and a separate balance sheet.[73]

13.4 Tax Considerations Arising on M&A Transactions

[189] There is no separate tax on capital gains under Uzbek legislation. Capital gains (on investments) are taxed at the usual corporate income tax rate.

[190] The Tax Code grants exemption from VAT on transactions (including sale) in securities and shares in respect of M&A transactions in JSCs and LLCs.

13.5 Structuring the Investment

13.5.1 Withholding Taxes

[191] The Uzbek-sourced income of a foreign legal entity (FLE) that is not attributable to a permanent establishment (PE) may be subject to withholding tax at source. For taxation purposes, an Uzbek entity or FLE with a registered PE which makes payments to an FLE without a PE should act as a tax agent. This implies an obligation to withhold tax from Uzbek-sourced income, as long as that income is not connected with an Uzbek PE. Failure to do so may lead to significant fines. Withholding tax is required to be withheld by residents of the Republic of Uzbekistan, as well as by non-residents of the country, i.e. by the PE.

[192] The Tax Code sets the following rates for withholding tax:

- dividends and interest – 10%;
- insurance premiums for contracts of insurance, coinsurance, and reinsurance – 10%;
- telecommunication for international connection, and international carriage (contracts on freight) – 6%;
- income received from the sale of shares, goods, rent and sub-rent of real estate, royalties, free-of-charge property, services (including management and consulting services) – 20%.

13.5.2 Double Taxation Treaty (DTT)

[193] Uzbekistan has entered into DTTs with fifty-two countries of the world.[74] Therefore, legal entities with Uzbek-sourced income that is not related to a PE can

---

[73] Tax Code, Art. 35.

[74] Austria, Azerbaijan, Bahrain, Belarus, Belgium, Bulgaria, Canada, China, Czech Republic, Estonia, Finland, France, Georgia, Germany, Greece, Hungary, India, Indonesia, Iran, Ireland, Israel, Italy,

benefit from a special deduction from the withholding tax rate. Each DTT establishes particular rates for the particular country.

13.5.3 Thin Capitalisation

[194] Currently, Uzbek legislation does not provide any rules on thin capitalisation.

13.5.4 Transfer Pricing

[195] The concept of transfer pricing has limited scope in Uzbekistan, according to the Tax Code. The tax authorities have the right to adjust revenue derived from a 'related party transaction' (related party transactions are those involving legal entities incorporated in Uzbekistan and their foreign founders/members/participants; or involving foreign legal persons and their founders/members/participants in Uzbekistan; as well as those between Uzbek and foreign legal entities which have common founders/participants/members) in order to reflect the market rate. However, due to a lack of guidance on the further application of the law, the interpretation of this regulation is unclear.

14 EMPLOYMENT CONSIDERATIONS

14.1 Legislative Framework

[196] In Uzbekistan, the Labour Code is the primary law regulating the interests of employees, employers and the state; fair and safe labour conditions; and the protection of labour rights and the health of workers. Furthermore, there are some other legal acts affecting labour and employment. The legislation on labour consists of the Labour Code, the laws of Uzbekistan, Resolutions of Parliament (Oliy Majlis) and Presidential Edicts.

14.2 Employment Protection

[197] The Labour Code, which was introduced on 1 April 1996, deals with labour legislation in the interests both of workers and employers and ensures the effective functioning of the labour market.

[198] Article 97 of the Labour Code covers the grounds for the termination of an employment contract. In accordance with Article 98 of the Labour Code, where

---

Japan, Jordan, Kazakhstan, Kuwait, Kyrgyzstan, Latvia, Lithuania, Luxembourg, Malaysia, Moldova, The Netherlands, Oman, Pakistan, Poland, Romania, Russia, Saudi Arabia, Singapore, Slovak Republic, Slovenia, South Korea, Spain, Switzerland, Thailand, Turkey, Turkmenistan, Ukraine, United Arab Emirates, United Kingdom, Vietnam.

there is a change of the owner of the enterprise, as well as a change due to its reorganisation (merger, division, transformation, or distribution), the employment relationship may continue with the consent of the employee. However, the new owner has the right to terminate the employment contracts of the head of the enterprise, his deputies, the chief accountant, and (in the absence of the position of chief accountant at the enterprise), of the employee performing the functions of the chief accountant. Termination of the employment contracts of other employees of the company is possible only in accordance with the legislation.

[199] In addition, it should be noted that in case of a change of ownership, collective agreements concluded between the company and its employees remain in force for a period of 6 months. Within this period, the parties are supposed to renegotiate it.

[200] There is no legal requirement to offer employees management representation (i.e. one or more seats on the Board) even in large companies. There are also no provisions or articles in the Labour Code giving employees the right to receive information or advice or to be consulted in connection with the acquisition of an enterprise.

[201] Uzbek legislation does not have the concept of a works council. Instead, there are representatives of the interests of employees and trade unions. Employees themselves determine the body to which they entrust their representation and the protection of their interests.

[202] All representative bodies operate within their powers and have equal rights to protect the interests of employees.

[203] The rights of trade unions and their elected bodies in relations with state and economic bodies and employers are determined by law,[75] statutes, collective agreements and other agreements.[76]

[204] Representative bodies of employees have the right:

- to negotiate and conclude collective agreements and other agreements, to monitor their implementation, to make proposals to the employer on the formulation of regulations governing working conditions at the enterprise;
- to participate in consideration of issues of social and economic development of the enterprise;
- to protect the interests of employees of authorities of the labour court;
- to appeal against decisions of the employer or of persons authorised by the employer if they contravene the legislation or other normative acts on labour or otherwise violate the rights of employees.[77]

[205] The exercise of the rights of representative bodies of employees should not reduce the efficiency of the enterprise or violate the established order and mode of its operation.

---

[75] The Law 'On Trade Unions' No. ZRU-588 dated 6 Dec. 2019.
[76] Article 22 of the Labour Code.
[77] Article 23 of the Labour Code.

[206] As mentioned above, Uzbek law does not provide for the consent of workers to any corporate transaction. As regards the dismissal of employees, the basis of termination of the employment contract on the initiative of the employer is provided for in Article 100 of the Labour Code of Uzbekistan.

[207] Employees whose employment contract is terminated[78] must be informed in person about the upcoming dismissal at least two months in advance. Also, not less than two months prior to implementation, employers are obliged to inform the employment authorities and trade unions about any mass redundancies or mass layoffs of workers.

[208] Employees dismissed due to a reduction in the number of staff are entitled to severance pay amounting to not less than the average BCR[79] and to further payments not less than the average BCR during the period of the job search (but not exceeding two months).

[209] Everyone is guaranteed the protection of labour rights, compliance with which is monitored by supervision and control, including by the bodies concerned with labour disputes. The Ministry of Employment and Labour Relations of Uzbekistan and its territorial bodies are responsible for the full implementation of the Labour Code.

[210] The Labour Code has separate chapters on the liability of parties to the labour contract. A party to a labour agreement (whether employer or employee) that has caused harm to the other party in connection with the performance of duties in the workplace is obliged to reimburse the injured party in accordance with the rules established by the Labour Code and other regulations on labour. Termination of employment after such harm has occurred does not entail exemption from the employment contract liability.[80]

[211] The employment contract may be terminated in cases specified in the labour code. These include:

- by agreement of the parties. On this basis, all types of employment contracts may be terminated at any time;
- on the initiative of one of the parties;
- upon expiry of the term;
- in circumstances beyond the control of the parties;
- on the grounds specified in the employment contract;
- in connection with non-election for a new term or refusal to participate in such election.

[212] The employer must notify the employee about his/her intention to terminate the employment agreement in written form. Prior notice must be given at least two months before the termination of the employment contract where termination is due to changes in the structure of the organisation, or at least two weeks before the

---

[78] Based on specified in Art. 100 of the Labour Code.
[79] Article 109 of the Labour Code.
[80] Article 185 of the Labour Code.

termination of the employment contract where termination is due to insufficient qualifications or health reasons. In such cases, the employer must pay compensation in the amount of two weeks' earnings.

[213] The Labour Code does not differentiate between workers. All the procedures must be applied equally, to both 'blue collar' as well as to 'white collar' workers.

Labour costs

[214] The legal duration of work is 40 hours per week.[81] Overtime hours should be no more than 4 hours for every two days or 120 hours per year.[82]

[215] In accordance with the Presidential Decree No. UP-5553 dated 13 October 2018 'On the Increase of Wages, Pensions, Scholarships, and Benefits' from 1 November 2018, the amount of wages, pensions, scholarships, and benefits has increased by an average of 1.1 times. The current BCR is UZS 202 730 (approximately USD 24).

14.3 Pensions

[216] In accordance with the law of Uzbekistan 'On the State Pension Provision of Citizens', a retirement pension is granted to insured employees on general grounds. Men can claim their retirement pension from the age of sixty, after a minimum period of twenty-five years of working, while women can claim upon reaching 55 years of age with a total length of service of not less than twenty years.[83]

[217] In addition to personal income tax, the employer is required to pay unified social payments, as referred to in section 14.2 above. The obligation to charge and withhold payments, as well as the responsibility for the correctness of the calculation lies on the employer.

14.4 Retention of Key Management and Employees

[218] The law does not provide for any mechanism to ensure the continuation (with the purchased entity) of the work of individual management team members or other key staff. According to the Labour Code, an employee has the right to terminate an employment contract concluded for an indefinite period, as well as a fixed-term employment contract before the expiration of its term, by notifying the employer in writing two weeks in advance. After the expiration of the period of warning, the employee has the right to stop work, and the employer is obliged to give the employee a workbook and to make a calculation with him. Therefore,

---

[81] Labour Code, Art. 115(1).
[82] Labour Code, Art. 125.
[83] Law No. 938-XII 'On State Pension Provision of Citizens' dated 3 Sep. 1993, Art. 7.

retention strategies used in the context of acquisitions tend to take the form of contractual obligations.

14.5 Treatment of Foreign Employees

[**219**] The main normative legal acts regulating the employment of foreign citizens in Uzbekistan are:

- The Labour Code
- Regulations on the procedure for the attraction and use of a foreign labour force in Uzbekistan ('**Regulation-244**');[84]
- Instruction on the procedure for application of Regulations on the procedure for the attraction and use of a foreign labour force in Uzbekistan, as approved by the Ministry of Labour ('**Instruction-285-3**').[85]

[**220**] Uzbek law does not contain restrictions on hiring foreign citizens as managers or directors. However, an Uzbek legal entity has to obtain permission to employ a foreign citizen as an employee or a director. To obtain permission, the employer must submit the necessary documents to the Agency for External Labour Migration under the Ministry of Labour and Social Protection ('**the Agency**').

[**221**] The Agency reviews the documents and issues a permit within thirty days from the date of submission of documents. The consideration of documents for qualified foreign specialists takes no more than fifteen working days. It is normally issued for six months to one year and can be further extended on a yearly basis.

[**222**] Subject to a permit, the employer enters into an employment contract with a foreign citizen, indicating the specific position for which he wants to attract the foreign specialist.

[**223**] Both parties sign the contract, and the employer (or his authorised representative) applies to the Agency for confirmation. If Uzbekistan has a visa regime with the country of citizenship of the foreign worker, for his/her entry into the territory of Uzbekistan for the purpose of employment, it is necessary to issue an employment visa, which is issued only after receiving confirmation. The prospective foreign employee will also need to acquire a Telex Number/Invitation Letter for a work visa from the host company, which must be approved by the authorities. Based on such approval, foreigners can apply for a visa.

[**224**] Foreign workers who have received confirmation are not entitled to work for any other employer. It is prohibited to transfer permission from one employer to another employer.

---

[84] Adopted by the Cabinet of Minister No. 244 dated 25 Mar. 2019.
[85] Approved by the Order of the Minister of Employment and Labour Relations of the Republic of Uzbekistan No. 285-3 dated 5 Aug. 2019.

[225] According to Article 11 of the Labour Code, foreign citizens and stateless persons working in the territory of Uzbekistan under employment contracts concluded with an employer are subject to labour legislation. This means that they enjoy labour rights and bear responsibilities on an equal basis with Uzbek citizens.

[226] Foreign citizens permanently residing in the territory of Uzbekistan are employed in the same manner as citizens of Uzbekistan. This category of foreign citizens is not subject to Regulation-408. For their employment, it is not necessary to obtain a prior permit for the engagement of foreign labour by a domestic employer, nor to obtain the foreign employee's confirmation of the right to work in Uzbekistan.

[227] The founders (participants) of an LLC have the right to appoint a foreign citizen permanently residing in the territory of Uzbekistan to the position of Director, with the conclusion of an employment contract for the term of his or her residence permit. It should also be noted that, when applying for a job, a foreign citizen permanently residing in Uzbekistan must present the documents listed in Article 80 of the Labour Code, as well as a residence permit issued by the internal affairs authorities at the place of residence.

[228] Once a foreign person arrives in Uzbekistan, he/she must register his/her stay in Uzbekistan within seventy-two hours after his/her arrival with the relevant internal affairs authorities. If a person stays in a hotel, it is the hotel's responsibility to register the person's stay for the period of his/her stay. If a person stays in a place other than a hotel, registration is to be arranged by the host company, and by the owner of the premises where the person is to stay, at the local department of the internal affairs authorities.

[229] Foreign employees require work permits to work for an Uzbek legal entity.[86] All individuals are taxed in Uzbekistan if they are considered 'resident' for tax purposes. In order to be considered 'resident', an individual should be physically present in Uzbekistan for 183 days or more in any period up to twelve months ending in a calendar year. Residents are taxed on their worldwide income, while non-residents are taxed only on their income originating from Uzbekistan.

[230] If an individual is considered a tax resident of Uzbekistan and of another country with which a treaty has been concluded, the resident may be entitled, based on the so-called 'rules that prevail over domestic tax legislation', to avoid double taxation. However, in order to apply the provisions of the treaty contract, the individual must be able to submit a residence certificate from his or her other country of residence confirming his/her resident status there.

---

[86] Law 'On approval of the Regulations on the Procedure for Attracting and Using Foreign Labour Power in the Republic of Uzbekistan' No. 244 dated 25 Mar. 2019.

15 ACCOUNTING TREATMENT

[231] The Law on Accounting[87] is the main law regulating accounting and reporting. There are also by-laws under this law, where the detailed requirements of the accounting report are given.

[232] In order to ensure the comparability of financial statements of the enterprises for different reporting periods, as well as of the financial statements of different enterprises, National Accounting Standard (NAS) No. 1 'Accounting policy and financial statements' establishes the basis for the formation and preparation of financial statements of enterprises.

[233] The law does not provide the format and content of reports for group accounts. In accordance with the Law on Accounting, accounting entities can apply international financial reporting standards.[88]

[234] The Law on Accounting does not specify any obligation to apply IFRS. However, Article 9 of the Presidential Edict[89] specifies that during 2015–2018 all JSCs must proceed to the publication of annual financial statements and conduct external audits in accordance with international standards on auditing and IFRS.

[235] Neither the Law on Accounting nor its by-laws consider the reorganisation of enterprises by merger as a separate type of activity. Based on this, we can say that there is no accounting definition of a merger or acquisition. In practice, expenses related to mergers and/or acquisitions are recorded and disclosed as 'other operating expenses'.

[236] Nonetheless, a consolidated financial statement must usually be submitted. In accordance with NAS No. 8, a parent company has to submit consolidated financial statements. However, if the parent company is itself a subsidiary owned by another company, it is not obliged by law to submit consolidated statements, provided that it is not otherwise required to do so by its parent company and provided there is consent to this from any minority shareowners.

[237] Any such parent company should disclose in separate financial statements the following:

- the reason for not presenting consolidated financial statements;
- the method used in the accounting for investments in a subsidiary;
- the name and registered office of its own parent company that does present consolidated financial statements.

[238] A parent company is also not required to prepare consolidated financial statements if it has only dependent companies. Each such case is subject to disclosure in the notes to the balance sheet and in the report on the financial results of the parent company.

---

[87] Law 'On Accounting' No. ZRU-404 dated 13 Apr. 2016.
[88] Article 10 of the Law 'On Accounting'.
[89] Law No. PD-4720 'On measures on introduction of modern methods of corporate management in joint-stock companies' dated 24 Apr. 2015.

[239] Under Uzbek legislation, when shares and other securities of a company are issued or placed, they may be paid for in cash or other means of payment such as property, as well as rights (including property) having a monetary value. Thus share-for-share acquisitions are technically feasible and provided for by law. However, in practice, this type of acquisition is rarely used. Thus, the accounting concept of 'merger relief' as used in many Western jurisdictions is not available by law and accordingly is not recognised by Uzbek law.

Goodwill and Intangible Assets

[240] Goodwill should not be recognised in the books of the acquiring company as an asset where it arises in the context of the purchase of an enterprise representing the difference between the purchase price and the actual book values of the relevant assets.

[241] The value of intangible assets is written down/ redeemed through amortisation. The amortised value is spread evenly over the useful life of the relevant asset in the form of amortisation expense of the enterprise.

[242] The amortisation of goodwill is recorded in accounting terms by reducing its cost over its useful life. The goodwill amortisation period should reflect the best estimate of the period during which future economic benefits are expected to flow to the enterprise. The useful life of goodwill must not exceed twenty years (or the expected life of the business, if less) from the date of initial recognition.

[243] The amortisation of goodwill has to be affected using the methods and, in the manner, provided for in paragraph 7 of NAS No. 7. In the financial statements, the value of goodwill is recorded net of the amortisation made during the reporting period.

[244] The useful life of intangible assets is determined based on:

- the term of the patent or other certificate and any other restrictions on the period of use of intangible assets in accordance with the legislation of Uzbekistan;
- the period during which the enterprise is expected to receive economic benefits (income) from their use.

[245] For individual groups of intangible assets, the useful life is determined based on the quantity of production or on some other natural measure of the amount of work expected to be derived from use of the intangible asset. For intangible assets for which it is impossible to determine the useful life, depreciation rates are set at five years.

[246] The useful life of intangible assets may not exceed the expected period of activity of the enterprise, starting from the moment of readiness of the intangible asset for use, unless otherwise provided by the legislation of Uzbekistan.

[247] NAS No. 7 defines the methodology of accounting for and recording of intangible assets [90] in the financial statements of the relevant entity. However, this does not apply to banks and other credit institutions in respect of their rights of ownership, economic management or operational management.

[248] The definition of intangible assets requires that the asset be used in business and must not have a physical existence. The asset meets the definition of an intangible asset when it has no physical existence, but it may be associated with legal rights, including the right of ownership, and it must be used over a long period of time.

[249] In order to enter intangible assets in the books of an enterprise it is necessary simultaneously to meet the following conditions:

- lack of material (physical) existence (form);
- the use of the asset in the production of goods, in the performance of work or services, or for administrative or other functions of the enterprise over a long period of time. At the same time, the cost of the asset must be not less than fifty times the BCR established in Uzbekistan. The head of the company has the right to set a lower limit on the value of assets for accounting purposes as part of intangible assets for the reporting year;
- the enterprise does not intend to resell the asset;
- reliability, including available documents evidencing the existence of the assets and the exclusive rights of the enterprise to such assets;[91]
- the possibility of identification.[92]

[250] According to the Law on Accounting, intangible assets are amortised. Property and intangible assets [93] are recognised as fixed assets and are accounted for by the taxpayer for tax purposes by depreciation and amortisation respectively in accordance with the Law on Accounting.

[251] Expenses on intangible assets are subject to deduction from total income in the form of depreciation on a monthly basis according to the norms calculated by the taxpayer based on their initial cost and useful life, but for no longer than the period of the taxpayer's activity.

[252] Determination of the useful life of intangible assets is based on the term of the patent, the certificate and (or) other restrictions on the conditions of use of intellectual property in accordance with the legislation of Uzbekistan or the applicable legislation of a foreign country, as well as on the useful life of intangible assets, taking account of any relevant contracts.

---

[90] NAS No. 7 defines intangible assets as 'identifiable objects of property that do not have material content, which the company keeps in order to use them in the production of products, works, services or sales of goods, or for the implementation of administrative and other functions for a long period.'

[91] Patients' certificates, other security documents, the contract of assignment (acquisition) of the patent, trademark, etc.

[92] Article 6 of the NAS No. 7.

[93] For the purpose of application of Art. 144 of the Tax Code.

[253] For intangible assets for which it is impossible to determine their useful life, depreciation rates are set based on five years, or (if less) the period of the taxpayer's activity.

[254] Goodwill generated from the purchase of an enterprise should not be recognised as an asset where it arises from the difference between the purchase price and the actual book values of the assets of the acquired enterprise.[94]

[255] According to NAS No. 7, the amount of goodwill acquired is determined by calculating the difference between the actual book values of the acquired items and the market value of the net assets (market value of assets less the amount of all liabilities) of the entity at the date of its purchase (acquisition). This should be treated as a price premium paid by the buyer in anticipation of future economic benefits and should be recorded as a separate inventory item.

[256] Any amount of negative goodwill should be considered as a discount on the price paid by the buyer due to the deficiency of factors such as stable buyers, quality reputation, marketing or sales skills, business relations, management experience, staff skills and so on, and should be considered as future income.

[257] In the financial statements, the value of goodwill is recorded net of the write-offs incurred during the reporting period. The amount of negative goodwill is attributed to the financial results of the entity as 'other income from operating activities' on a systematic basis over the weighted average useful life of the identified depreciable assets which have been acquired.

[258] In accordance with NAS No. 23, it is recommended to draw up a transfer deed or separation balance sheets to coincide with the end of the reporting period (year) or with the date of any interim financial statements which provide the basis for evaluating the transferred assets and liabilities of the reorganised enterprise.

16 FUTURE DEVELOPMENTS

[259] In February 2017, the government adopted Presidential Decree No. UP-4947 on Uzbekistan's Strategy for Further Development.[95] The objective of the Strategy for 2017–2021 is to raise the efficiency of governmental reforms, to create conditions for ensuring comprehensive and accelerated development of the state and society, and to establish the priority sectors for the country's modernisation and liberalisation. The liberalisation of the foreign exchange market, as well as the transition to inflation targeting, modernisation of the agriculture sector, and improvements to the quality of education and healthcare services were all considered in the Development Strategy of Uzbekistan for 2017–2021.

[260] The government pays special attention to the development and modernisation of infrastructure. A number of infrastructure development and modernisation

---

[94] Article 62 of NAS No. 7.
[95] Decree of the President of the Republic of Uzbekistan 'On the Strategy of Action for the Further Development of the Republic of Uzbekistan' No. 4947 dated 7 Feb. 2017.

programmes have been adopted in recent years, specifically in engineering communications and road transport, which are planned to be completed in 2019.

[261] Based on the progress achieved by the government, the World Bank named Uzbekistan as one of the top ten global improvers in 2017.

[262] We anticipate that a number of government initiatives could potentially act as catalysts for further M&A activity in Uzbekistan during the coming few years. These initiatives include the following:

[263] In September 2018, the Presidential Decree 'On Approval of the Strategy of Innovative Development of the Republic of Uzbekistan for 2019–2021' was adopted.[96] This Decree aims to develop the country's innovation potential and to identify the main barriers which currently exist to innovation in the Republic. One of the main goals of the strategy is for Uzbekistan to rank in the top fifty in the Global Innovation Index by 2030;

[264] Tax Reform is one of the most important projects in Uzbekistan. In February 2018, the President signed the Resolution 'On Organisational Measures for Cardinal Improvement of Tax Legislation'.[97] In accordance with this Presidential Resolution, the government established the Tax Concept, which focuses on new reforms designed to improve tax regulations. The new Tax Code is aimed at, amongst other objectives, better administration of taxation and improvement of the investment climate. The new Tax Code is due to be approved in early 2019.

Privatisation

[265] Uzbekistan has a comprehensive privatisation programme designed to reduce state involvement in the economy by way of the sale of assets of state enterprises. On 28 April 2015, the President of the Republic of Uzbekistan approved a programme to increase the share of the private sector in the economy. This provides for the transfer of 1,247 enterprises and assets over to private ownership. As a result, the number of privatised entities has increased as follows: in 2014 (288), 2015 (848), 2016 (609), 2017 (542) and as at September 2018 (541).[98]

[266] The government has also undertaken measures for the sale of empty, low-liquidity state-owned facilities at a 'zero' purchase price to expand participation of the private sector in the economy and to provide conditions for the creation of new jobs. Below are examples of successful privatisations under government initiatives.

[267] JV LLC 'UZTEX Shovot' located in the Shavat district of the Khorezm region was purchased at a 'zero' purchase price subject to a requirement to launch modern textile production at the site, including completion of a spinning mill. The purchaser invested over USD28.5m and created over 380 new jobs.

[268] LLC 'Roison Electronics', was an investment in accordance with an Agreement on the Sale-Purchase of the Stocks Package of JSC 'Algoritm' which took the

---

96 No. UP-5544 dated 21 Sep. 2018.
97 No. UP5116 dated 18 Jul. 2017.
98 According to the State Committee of the Republic of Uzbekistan on Statistics.

form of an arrangement to manufacture household appliances. Currently, more than USD21m has been invested and over 100 new jobs created.

[269] LLC 'BF Textile Production' in Tashkent city – the buildings and facilities of the bankrupt 'UzbekTextileMash' enterprise were privatised for UZS5.4bn and an additional USD19.2m was invested in modernisation, resulting in over 300 new jobs.

[270] The government is also considering privatisations in other state-owned sectors in the coming years. In this respect, we would like to bring the following findings to your attention:

[271] In 2018, the President approved the gradual reduction of the state's share in the electric power industry by attracting private capital. In December 2018, the relevant authorities began to form and approve a list of enterprises recommended for transfer to private hands based on a public-private partnership. A technical and financial audit is planned for April 2019 to assess the status of enterprises on this list, and by June 2019 the government will, in conjunction with international consultants, prepare technical specifications for the development of tender documentation.

[272] In May 2018 it was reported that Uzbekistan was ready to privatise its national airline, Uzbekistan Airways. The government is currently in cooperation with the World Bank to reform the country's aviation sector so that Uzbekistan Airways is withdrawn from the list of inviolable companies.

[273] JSC Uzavtosanoat has attracted foreign investors to the JSC Jizzakh Accumulator Plant. In accordance with the Presidential Resolution of the Republic of Uzbekistan 'On measures for the further development of JSC Jizzakh Accumulator Plant' No. PP-3773 dated 5 June 2018, JSC Uzavtosanoat placed 51.78% of its shares in the JSC Dzhizak Accumulator Plant for sale to foreign investors through the brokerage company JSC Mulk-Sarmoya Brokerlik Uyi. Shares were issued for sale to foreign investors on 14 December 2018.

[274] The government has also decided to rehabilitate other large state-owned enterprises through the sale of shares on the stock exchange. In early January 2018, it became known that the Chinese company Xuzhou Construction Machinery Co Ltd would buy a 51% stake in the Urgench Excavator plant. The shares were issued the following May.

[275] Additionally, JSC Uzavtosanoat has placed for sale state-owned shares in three dealer enterprises. Shares of dealers placed in various regions will be put up for auction through the organiser – LLC Respublika Mulk Markazi – for sale to private entrepreneurs.

[276] In November 2018, the first SPO in the history of Uzbekistan was launched – a collection of applications from investors for the purchase of shares of the Kokand Mechanical Plant. The decision to enter and list the Kokand Mechanical Plant on the stock exchange was taken by the government as part of its national strategy for the privatisation of enterprises. The SPO plans to sell 2.2 m shares, which will reduce the share of Uzneftegazmash to 64.08% and will increase the share of other shareholders to 35.92%. Uzneftegazmash will use the funds received to update, expand and modernise its enterprises, as well as to expand into new markets.